D1091239

# Multinational Corporations and East European Socialist Economies

# Geza P. Peter Lauter
# Paul M. Dickie

# Multinational Corporations and East European Socialist Economies

PRAEGER SPECIAL STUDIES IN INTERNATIONAL ECONOMICS AND DEVELOPMENT

**Praeger Publishers**    New York    Washington    London

Library of Congress Cataloging in Publication Data

Lauter, Geza Peter.
    Multinational corporations and East European socialist
economies.

    (Praeger special studies in international economics
and development)
    Bibliography: p.
    Includes index.
    1. International business enterprises.  2.  Europe,
Eastern—Economic conditions.   I.  Dickie, Paul M.,
joint author.   II.  Title.
HD69.I7L33      1975        338.8'8'0943          74-333
ISBN 0-275-09250-X

PRAEGER PUBLISHERS
111 Fourth Avenue, New York, N.Y. 10003, U.S.A.

Published in the United States of America in 1975
by Praeger Publishers, Inc.

Printed in the United States of America

To Eva-Maria and Carole

One of the more interesting developments of East-West trade in general and East-West industrial cooperation in particular is the increasing participation of multinational corporations throughout Eastern Europe in projects ranging from complex, equity-based joint ventures (Control Data Corporation in Romania), to simple contract manufacturing. What makes this development so interesting is that until recently the Eastern European socialist governments considered multinational corporations the prototype of aggressive Western business organizations that were developed for the sole purpose of furthering the imperialist aims of Western, especially American, capitalists throughout the world. Such rigid ideological views were based on political considerations that precluded the development of closer economic ties between multinationals and the Eastern European countries.

The easing of political tensions the world over created a more conducive atmosphere for the development of economic ties during the 1970s. Moreover, as a result of the switch from extensive to intensive economic growth--the more efficient utilization of existing plants and labor as opposed to the addition of new plants and labor--the socialist countries developed a great need for advanced technology, access to hard currency markets, and generally increased industrial efficiency. By virtue of their size, scope of activities, control over technology, and markets, multinational corporations are best qualified to satisfy these needs.

This study is concerned with the reasons for and the problems of the emerging close economic ties between multinational corporations and the Eastern European socialist economies. Because this relationship is at a very early stage, not many detailed examples could be obtained to support the various points made. In this sense, many of the ideas and propositions developed throughout the study should be viewed as tentative explanations to be tested in the near future when--assuming stable worldwide political and economic conditions--numerous examples of close economic ties between multinational corporations and the Eastern European socialist economies will be more readily available.

The emerging relationship is referred to in this study as "close economic ties." As such, this term includes all forms of East-West trade and, more important, all forms of East-West industrial cooperation as identified in the 1973 report of the UN Economic Commission for Europe.

There is no generally accepted definition of multinational corporations. (Consequently, multinationals are understood throughout the book as "enterprises that conduct substantial business in more than two countries." The Eastern European socialist economies included are Bulgaria, Czechoslovakia, the German Democratic Republic, Hungary, Poland, and Romania. In the strict sense, the German Democratic Republic cannot be called an Eastern European nation. However, it is treated as such in reference to the status ascribed to it by the mutual political and economic treaties, such as the Warsaw Pact and the Council for Mutual Economic Assistance (CMEA) in which it participates. Yugoslavia, because of its unique political and economic position merits a special study and is, consequently, excluded.

The book is based on the exploration of Western and Eastern European secondary sources, such as government publications, academic studies, books and articles as well as on interviews in the field held with managers of multinational corporations, Eastern European economic policy makers, and academicians.

LIST OF TABLES AND FIGURE

xi

# Multinational Corporations and East European Socialist Economies

# 1

## MULTINATIONAL
## CORPORATIONS

The advent of modern multinational corporations has distorted the long-standing concepts of international trade and finance. International trade theory holds that if a nation specializes in the production of goods with low relative cost, it can obtain through trade goods whose relative domestic production costs are high. Given such specialization, national income can be substantially higher than if a full range of goods were produced domestically. Under traditional theory, capital and labor are assumed to be nontraded factors of production. However, the dominance of multinationals came about through specialization that transcends national borders and was made possible by large movements of factors of production, particularly capital, from one country to another.

Today no nation can expect to dispose of its domestic surplus by simply offering it for sale in international markets. While some commodities, such as agricultural products or minerals, can still be traded in this manner, their proportion in total world trade has markedly declined. Moreover, the nations producing such commodities want to provide their domestic economies with the additional employment and profit opportunities made possible by further processing and manufacturing. Consequently, competition in world markets is continually increasing and sophisticated marketing has become a necessity in international trade. Multinational corporations have the expertise and channels of distribution needed for the global marketing of large volumes of manufactured goods. They are also involved in the design and manufacture stage of the production process; thus, their worldwide expansion was a natural development.

The expansion of multinational corporations has resulted in large flows of factors of production across national boundaries not envisioned in traditional trade
theory. Both capital and labor have become very mobile.
As a result, in most of the world today, multinational
corporations are seen as one of the major factors promoting
economic development. At the same time, these international
flows have contributed to severe disruptions in the international financial markets as well as in the social fabric
of several countries. To better understand the current
role and influence of multinationals, the following section
presents a brief review of their emergence.


## HISTORICAL REVIEW

Multinationals, except for their legal form, are not
a new phenomenon. Using the definition presented in the
Preface, "enterprises that conduct substantial business
in two or more countries," they date back at least 3,000
years before Christ to Mesopotamia.[1] The Mesopotamian
businessmen or <u>damkars</u> had a well-developed system of
business contacts including joint stock companies. Their
activities encompassed trade in such items as wool, spices,
bronze, and slaves, and also involved the setting up of
colonies in Asia and possibly Western Europe. With the
successful working of iron around 1,000 B.C., Mesopotamian
industries provided the then-known world with the sword as
well as with improved domestic implements. In terms of
power and influence these companies rivaled their modern
counterparts. There is, however, a difference.

To understand this difference it is important to remember that in the era of European imperialism, the 17th
and 18th centuries, nation states rose in prominence
through the amalgamation of the previously self-ruled
cities. The sovereigns of these newly emerged nations
were absolutists and, following in the footsteps of the
previous city-based business oligarchs, entered commerce
to obtain wealth and power.

> Soon Europe was full of kings in business as it
> had formerly been of millionaires manipulating
> kings. Instead of a Jacob Fugger shaping the
> policies of the Habsburgs in his countinghouse,
> there was presented a still more entertaining
> spectacle of a Bourbon monarch presiding, if
> with rather ill grace, over a shareholders' as-

sembly of the French East Indian Company. Where once merchants had ruled their city-states in the interests of business, there now appeared sovereigns who sought to control and turn business to the interest of the state.[2]

The entry of royalty into commerce was not limited to the home country, but had also been extended abroad. During this era, numerous companies were formed that were controlled by European royal families but that operated elsewhere in the world, for example, the Dutch East India Company, the Royal African Company, the Virginia Company, and the West India Company. An example of an enterprise that originated in this imperialist era but that survived to be a modern multinational is the Hudson's Bay Company of Canada.

The Hudson's Bay Company is North America's oldest company.[3] It was founded in 1670 with the backing of Prince Rupert, a cousin of King Charles II. The entrepreneurs that initiated it were two Frenchmen, Pierre Rodisan and Medart Chouart, from Three Rivers, Quebec. In 1660 these men had been victimized by the colonial French government in their fur trading activities and, failing to obtain redress from France, turned to England. Following an initial voyage to obtain beaver pelts on the shores of the Hudson's Bay in 1668, they, along with Price Rupert and other associates, were given a charter that entitled the company to control the entire watershed of the Hudson's Bay and by way of enforcement, to raise any army, build forts and operate ships of war. In total the company controlled 1,486,000 square miles or almost one-sixth of North America. In payment for this charter, the company undertook to discover the Northwest Passage and, as a homage of questionable value, to provide a pair of elk and beaver to any visiting monarch from England. The company founded outposts along the shore of the Hudson's Bay and through excellent relations with the Indians, trade grew rapidly and profitably.

In the period from 1690 to 1760 the company was heavily involved in the French-English wars that took place to determine the fate of North American colonies. In 1697, the Hudson's Bay Company's ships fought the French in an arctic naval action. The company ships lost and under the Treaty of Ryswick, the French took over their territories. However, in the War of Spanish Succession, the British were victorious and the Treaty of Utrecht in 1713 gave the Hudson's Bay back to England. The struggle between the French and the English fur traders continued unabated until the final capture of Montreal by Wolfe in 1760, which marked the end of the French presence in North America.

The Hudson's Bay Company changed from an agent of imperialism to an independent corporation when the Dominion of Canada was formed in 1867. The company's territory was admitted into the new confederation essentially via the Canadian government's purchase of the land for £300,000. The company retained land around each of its posts and a total of 7 million acres of fertile prairie land that was sold to settlers. Upon sale of these lands to settlers, the company retained the mineral rights that formed the basis for the present subsidiary companies, Hudson's Bay Resources and the Hudson's Bay Oil and Gas. Also, the trading post concept, so well developed by the Hudson's Bay Company, led to the development of a large network of department stores throughout Canada.

The modern Hudson's Bay Company is a diverse multinational. While it does not make _Fortune_'s lists of the largest non-U.S.-based multinationals, sales in 1972 amounted to $672 million on total assets of $419 million.[4] It has substantial operations in three countries--Canada, the United Kingdom, and the United States--with products as diverse as textiles and natural gas. Thus, the instrument of English economic imperialism became a large multinational corporation with little or no direct control by governments over its activities.

The change in multinational government relations over time is depicted in Figure 1. In the case of imperialism where business serves as an agent of imperialism, all lines of control and influence converge on the colony, either directly from the colonizer or through the business. In the modern setting, lines of influence are relatively weak between governments (international agreements, bilateral agreements, and other more informal channels) while each government controls the boundaries of business activities without directly controlling business operations (except in socialist economies). Modern multinationals with almost complete control over their subsidiaries can often weaken individual government controls through compensating actions--an issue to be discussed later. Moreover, as mentioned before, multinational corporations can be important agents of economic development (jobs, investment, training) and host countries often compete to attract subsidiaries, thereby reducing the potential for uniform controls.

FIGURE 1

Multinational Corporation--Government Relations

(a) <u>Age of Imperialism</u>

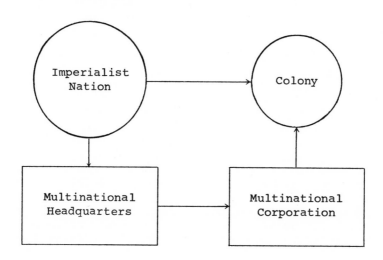

(b) <u>Modern</u>

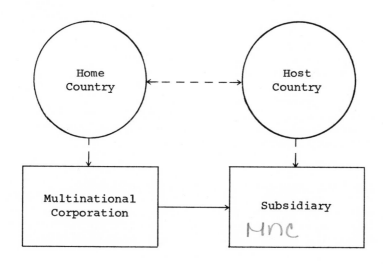

## ECONOMIC SIGNIFICANCE

It was only during the late 1960s that multinational corporations achieved preeminence throughout most of the nonsocialist world. As pointed out before, a large part of this importance derived from the gradual weakening of governmental influence over their activities.*

Statistical measurement of multinationals is extremely difficult. The reasons for this are the international nature of their operations, which are only partially and unevenly captured in the data reported by individual countries, and the relatively short period of time in which interest has focused on their activities.[5] The historical growth of multinationals, for example, can only be partially measured by looking at foreign direct investment by selected individual countries. In the 1958-71 period, U.S. direct foreign investment rose at the annual rate of 9 percent, that of Japan by 20 percent, and that of Canada by 8 percent. During the shorter time span of 1961-71, U.K. foreign direct investment increased at an annual rate of 11 percent, while that of the Federal Republic of Germany rose by 22 percent.

These generally very high growth rates were attributed to the rising levels of income in Europe following postwar reconstruction, the dollar surplus arising from the U.S. balance-of-payment deficits, the lessening of trade and investment barriers, and to the generally outward-looking behavior of business.

Perhaps the most comprehensive statistical description of the economic significance of multinational corporations is shown in Table 1.1. According to the data presented, foreign direct investment by the United States accounted for 55 percent of the total in 1967, followed by the United Kingdom with 16 percent, and France with 6 percent. In the period ending 1971, the shares contributed by the United States and the United Kingdom declined (to 52 percent and 15 percent, respectively) while that of Germany, Japan, Belgium, and Sweden rose markedly. This indicates that increasingly the sovereign base of multinationals is itself becoming more multinational.

---

*In this connection it should be remembered that, while both North and South American countries achieved independence at comparatively early dates, India did not achieve self-government until 1947, while many of the African colonies remained under foreign control until the 1960s.

TABLE 1.1

Market Economies:   Stock of Foreign Direct Investment,
1967 and 1971
(book value)

| Country[a] | 1967 Millions of Dollars | 1967 Percentage Share | 1971[b] Millions of Dollars | 1971[b] Percentage Share |
|---|---|---|---|---|
| United States | 59,486 | 55.0 | 86,001 | 52.0 |
| United Kingdom | 17,521 | 16.2 | 24,019 | 14.5 |
| France | 6,000 | 5.5 | 9,540 | 5.8 |
| Federal Republic of Germany | 3,015 | 2.8 | 7,276 | 4.5 |
| Switzerland | 4,250[c] | 3.9 | 6,760 | 4.1 |
| Canada | 3,728 | 3.4 | 5,930 | 3.6 |
| Japan | 1,458 | 1.3 | 4,480[d] | 2.7 |
| Netherlands | 2,250 | 2.1 | 3,580 | 2.2 |
| Sweden[e] | 1,514 | 1.4 | 3,450 | 2.1 |
| Italy | 2,110[f] | 1.9 | 3,350 | 2.0 |
| Belgium | 2,040[f] | 0.4 | 3,250 | 2.0 |
| Australia | 380[f] | 1.9 | 610 | 0.4 |
| Portugal | 200[f] | 0.2 | 320 | 0.2 |
| Denmark | 190[f] | 0.2 | 310 | 0.2 |
| Norway | 60[f] | 0.0 | 90 | 0.0 |
| Austria | 30[f] | 0.0 | 40 | 0.0 |
| Other[g] | 4,000[g] | 3.7 | 6,000 | 3.6 |
| Total | 108,200 | 100.0 | 165,000 | 100.0 |

[a]Countries are arranged in descending order of book value of direct investment in 1971.

[b]Estimated (except for United States, United Kingdom, Federal Republic of Germany, Japan, and Sweden) by applying the average growth rate of the United States, United Kingdom, and Federal Republic of Germany between 1966 and 1971.

[c]Data from another source for 1965 ($4,052 million) and 1969 ($6,043 million) seem to indicate that the 1967 and 1971 figures are probably relatively accurate.  See Max Ikle, Die Schweiz als internationaler Bank und Finanzplatz (Zurich, 1970).

[d]Financial Times, June 4, 1973.

[e]The figures for Sweden are for 1965 and 1970 instead of 1967 and 1971 and they are in current prices for total assets of majority-owned manufacturing subsidiaries.

[f]Data on book value of foreign direct investment are only available for developing countries.  Since the distribution of the minimum number of affiliates between developing countries and developed market economies correlates highly with the distribution of book value, the total book value has been estimated on the basis of the distribution of their minimum number of affiliates.  For Australia, the average distribution of the total minimum number of affiliates has been applied.

[g]Estimated, including developing countries.

Source:  Multinational Corporations and World Development (New York:  United Nations, 1973), p. 2.

Another set of data, shown in Table 1.2, presents a comparison between the 1971 foreign sales of the subsidiaries of multinational corporations and the 1971 exports of the countries in which the multinationals were based. In terms of this rough comparison, the sales of the subsidiaries of U.S.-based multinationals, estimated at $172 billion, far outweighed the total U.S. exports of $43.5 billion. While the same general relationship held for the United Kingdom, for most other countries exports exceeded the sales of subsidiaries of multinational corporations. It needs to be pointed out, however, that in total, estimated sales from production abroad by foreign subsidiaries exceeds world trade.*

The relationship between the production of multinational corporations and the GNP of national economies reinforces their economic importance. The value added by the top 10 multinational corporations in 1971 each exceeded $3 billion (if we assume total value added is about three-quarters of sales) and at this level, all 10 would have had production greater than 80 countries. Taken together, the value added by all multinational corporations has been estimated in 1971 to exceed $550 billion, or about one-fifth of the world's GNP, exclusive of the centrally planned economies.[6]

PATTERNS OF INTERNATIONAL EXPANSION

As indicated before, the activities of multinational corporations first developed in response to the global demand for raw materials. The worldwide investment pattern of oil companies--culminating in the 1950s--illustrates this point well. While the exploration for raw materials is likely to continue, the manufacturing activities of multinationals have increased in importance accounting for over 40 percent of the total estimated current foreign investment. On the other hand, oil accounts for 29 percent, mining and smelting for 7 percent, and other industries for 24 percent.[7]

---

*Foreign trade and sales by foreign subsidiaries are not directly comparable. Foreign subsidiary sales include domestic sales in the host country as well as sales to external markets. However, in relation to each country the level of exports versus foreign sales by subsidiaries gives some measure of the importance of MNCs within the external sector.

TABLE 1.2

Multinational Corporations in the World Economy, 1971
(billions of U.S. dollars)

| Country | Direct Investment Abroad | Sales from Production Abroad | Total Export of Country |
|---|---|---|---|
| United States | 86.0 | 172.0 | 43.5 |
| Britain | 24.0 | 48.0 | 22.4 |
| France | 9.5 | 19.1 | 20.4 |
| West Germany | 7.3 | 14.5 | 39.0 |
| Switzerland | 6.8 | 13.5 | 5.7 |
| Canada | 5.9 | 11.9 | 17.6 |
| Japan | 4.5 | 9.0 | 24.0 |
| Netherlands | 3.6 | 7.2 | 13.9 |
| Sweden | 3.5 | 6.9 | 7.5 |
| Italy | 3.4 | 6.7 | 15.1 |
| Belgium | 3.3 | 6.5 | 12.4 |
| Other | 7.4 | 14.7 | 90.4 |
| Total | 165.0 | 330.0 | 311.9 |

Source: Column 1 from Table 1.1; column 2 data estimated on the basis of a turnover ratio of 2.0; and column
3 data from International Monetary Fund, International Financial Statistics, April 1974.

Whereas most of the investments in resource industries
have been in the developing countries, manufacturing activities have been centralized, at least until recently,
in the industrial world. The so-called "runaway plants"
have emerged as an important factor only during the last
few years. Because of severe cost pressures in the industrialized world, multinationals have been increasingly at-
tracted to low labor-cost countries for the manufacture of
labor-intensive products as, for example, ready-to-wear
clothing, computer memory cores, and toys.[8] These products are manufactured in areas such as Korea, Taiwan,
Puerto Rico, and Hong Kong and are exported to industrialized markets. Although it has mainly been the U.S.-based
multinational corporations that have engaged in such investments, European multinationals are rapidly following
the trend due to the labor shortages and difficulties associated with their "guest-workers."

9

With the increased internationalization of manufacturing, there has been an increasing opportunity for the service industries to do likewise. Banking, advertising, legal services, and consulting are rapidly becoming multinational. In large measure this has developed in response to the growing multinational nature of their domestic producer clients. However, in many cases their growth has expanded much beyond providing overseas services to multinationals with the same home base. Between 1965 and 1972, U.S. banks more than tripled their foreign locations while foreign deposits of the large New York banks rose dramatically to a level of almost two-thirds of total domestic deposits.[9] In the advertising field U.S.-based companies have achieved similar growth. On the other hand, it appears that the consulting and legal services, after expanding rapidly in the 1960s, have slowed down overseas expansion.[10] The overseas expansion of non-U.S. service industries has probably paralleled the American experience, although at a somewhat slower pace.

To assess the performance and potential net benefits of multinational corporations it is necessary to review the theoretical propositions advanced to explain their expansion. These propositions, of which there is a growing number, can be segregated into two broad categories: those related to comparative advantages and associated with the more traditional view of profit maximization, and those related to markets and associated with sales maximization behavior. Underlying the arguments in both categories is maximization under the conditions of risk aversion. Concerning the comparative advantage-based propositions, several theorists view foreign investments as one of the alternative means of maximizing return on assets within the framework of a changing world environment.[11] This can be accomplished in part quite simply (at least theoretically) through gains from diversification. However, considering more fundamental factors, it is also reasonable in many cases to view the transfer of technology as the essence of foreign investment.[12] In order to maximize returns, multinational corporations holding a near monopoly on a given body of knowledge expand their operations outside the home-base country. The form of foreign investment can vary depending on the competitive conditions in the market, and the technology transfer method (licensing, patent sale, direct investment) can be selected so as to obtain the highest possible return. While these theoretical propositions are plausible, they are inadequate as comprehensive explanations. Nevertheless, they serve an important func-

tion in giving more substance to market-related propositions.

Market-related propositions explain international ex-
pansion--taking into account the dynamics of the products
and services sold--through sales maximization behavior under imperfect market conditions.  Dunning classifies international operations based on this type of market involvement in the following manner:  backward vertical integration involving the sourcing of raw materials, forward vertical integration involving the selling to foreign markets,
and horizontal integration involving the incorporation of
global facilities to achieve gains from complete international specialization.[13]  Within the context of forward
vertical integration, Vernon proposed the "product life
cycle" concept.  Given a standard domestic product life
cycle--introduction, growth, maturity, saturation, and
decline--he hypothesized that as the growth of domestic
sales begins to decline, producers start exploring foreign
markets.  With an increase in exports, certain markets become sufficiently developed to support production facilities.  Without foreign investment to supply the facilities,
the producers could lose the market to a host country firm.
This process continues from one area of the world to the
next until it is worldwide, then the product life cycle has
achieved maturity and begins to decline.  The case of manual Singer sewing machines is an apt illustration.  Introduced in the 1800s, the manual machines are still considered very valuable in parts of Africa where electricity is
unavailable or unreliable.  In fact, in some countries the
manual machines have not yet reached the maturity stage
in the product life cycle.

It should, of course, be recognized that this process
of international vertical integration as well as the other
variants are only possible if the producer has a comparative advantage in technology that it is willing to exploit.
Nevertheless, the driving force for expansion into international markets is sales maximization providing, of course,
that a minimum level of profits can be earned under the
general conditions of risk aversion.

The strategy that is developed for international expansion is largely dependent on the comparative advantage
multinational corporations have in conjunction with risk
aversion considerations.  If technology is the main factor of the multinationals' comparative advantage then licensing provides a relatively risk-free method of market
entry.  However, if multinational corporations also have
a comparative advantage in management (as, for example,

IBM) then, to fully exploit this factor they are likely to
seek expansion through wholly owned subsidiaries.  Moreover, the strategy also depends on the type of business
community in the host country.  For example, an active
business community often permits the use of joint venture
or licensing.  It is important to remember, however, that
the strategy used not only influences the attitudes of the
host government and citizens, but can also modify the behavior of the multinationals themselves.


CONTROL OF MULTINATIONALS

The impact of multinational corporations on the world
economy should be assessed in conjunction with an overview
of the effectiveness of international and national controls
over the activities of multinationals.

Multinationals with extensive operations in many countries can, through offsetting actions, effectively thwart
controls individual nations seek to impose.  As a result,
the burden of controls is placed on multilateral agreements
between nations.  However, the existing multilateral agreements were predicated on the control of trade and finance
in a world that did not include multinational corporations
as an integral part of the global economy.


General Agreement on
Tariffs and Trade

The General Agreement on Tariffs and Trade (GATT) was
founded under the general auspices of the United Nations.
This informal arrangement, designed as a framework for multilateral trade and tariff negotiations, replaced the International Trade Organization (ITO) that was rejected by
the U.S. Senate following World War II.  Consequently,
ITO never got beyond the planning stage.  While all the
provisions of ITO were adopted by GATT, ratification by
the U.S. Congress was not sought with the result that, although the United States has participated in the periodic
conferences concerning the reduction of tariffs, GATT has
never been officially recognized by the United States.

GATT, with a total of 83 contracting countries, seeks
to set and regulate the code of conduct for international
trade.[14]  The code includes the following:  the principle
of nondiscrimination, the prohibition of nontariff protection (except for those means that are designed to deal

with temporary balance-of-payments problems), and the principle of consultative exploration of damage to trade interests of member countries. Special provisions deal with the unique problems of developing countries. While these principles and procedures have had a generally beneficial effect on trade, the organization's main impact has been through the periodic negotiations for tariff reduction. Since the end of World War II there have been six major conferences to negotiate tariff concessions. The last one was the Kennedy Round (1962-67), which achieved tariff reduction on industrial goods of about 35 percent.

The principle of nondiscrimination in levying tariff duties is embodied in the most-favored-nations (MFN) clause. As adopted by GATT, the MFN clause is unconditional, that is, any tariff concession granted initially on a bilateral basis must be extended to all other member countries. There are, however, important exceptions to this principle. These include customs unions (EEC), free trade areas (EFTA), and other concessions such as the Commonwealth preferences instituted by the United Kingdom or the preferences given by the EEC to the former French and Belgian colonies. Although the clause does limit widespread discrimination, occasionally the basic principle is violated, as in the United States/Canada Auto Pact and the preferential concessions given to Tunisia and Morocco by the EEC. In the last few years all of the Eastern European socialist economies, with the exception of the German Democratic Republic and Bulgaria, have become members of GATT. For the socialist countries whose tariffs are not a major instrument of foreign trade control, the contracting parties of GATT have agreed to a gradual elimination of quantitative restrictions (defined in terms of growth in imports from other contracting members).[15] However, as specified under Article 35 of the GATT Charter, MFN treatment can be withheld from new members. For example, at the present time the United States only extends MFN treatment to Poland. Thus, discriminatory tariffs and other quantitative restrictions still remain an impediment to East-West trade.

The current Tokyo round of negotiations formally got under way in September 1973. The main purpose of this round of negotiations is to reduce nontariff barriers.[16] Working groups on tariffs, nontariff and other barriers, and agricultural as well as tropical products have been established. The working groups do statistical and analytical work to prepare the necessary information for the planned negotiations. There is, however, nothing on the

13

agenda dealing with trade between the subsidiaries of multinational corporations or on other related matters. GATT's emphasis continues to be on the outmoded concept of international trade according to which such trade can best be promoted through the mutual reduction of national barriers.

## International Monetary Fund

The International Monetary Fund (IMF) was founded at the Bretton Woods Conference of 1944 and, like GATT, is one of the foundations of post-World War II economic cooperation. The major purpose of the IMF was to promote and support an exchange rate system based on par values as well as to seek a reduction of exchange and trade restrictions. While the former purpose has been subsumed in the present discussions of international monetary reform, the latter purpose has a continued high level of support.

Members of the IMF now total 126 and include most of the nations of the world outside the socialist bloc (Yugoslavia and Romania are the only two Eastern European members). With membership, a country is assigned a quota payable 75 percent in local currency and 25 percent in gold (gold payments have increasingly been waived in favor of an equivalent amount of foreign exchange).* Member countries consult with the IMF concerning exchange rates so as to prevent competitive devaluations as experienced in the 1930s. In support of approved policies, the IMF can make foreign exchange resources available to individual countries. With increasing amounts of resources provided by the IMF relative to a country's quota, the degree of conditionality increases. Voting power in the IMF is based on proportional representation as determined by the relative size of quota so that the industrialized countries dominate the institution.

In the 1969-73 period the international monetary system was radically changed by two major events. First, the IMF itself instituted Special Drawing Rights (SDR's) to augment existing international reserves. In the three years ending 1971, 9.5 billion SDR's were allocated to individual countries; individual shares were based on the

---

*Quotas are based on a complex formula, including GNP, level of foreign trade, and fluctuations therein, as well as the magnitude of international reserves.

14

relative size of quotas. The creation of this reserve asset through international agreement laid one of the corner-
stones for the proposed reform. Second, the large volume
of international capital flows put unprecedented pressure
on the par value system until its collapse. This process
started with the Smithsonian Agreement in August 1971 at
which time the United States effectively devaluated the
dollar. The role of multinational corporations in these
large capital flows is a controversial subject. However,
it is clear that multinationals with exposure in a weak
currency take defensive actions to reduce that exposure.
If views concerning currencies become uniform with a substantial number of multinationals, the added pressures on
a currency can easily overwhelm any given country's foreign
exchange resources. In a study of multinational corporations by the U.S. Tariff Commission, it was estimated that
liquid assets of multinationals (including foreign branches
of banks) totaled some $268 billion in 1971.[17] In compari-
son, as of the same date, total foreign exchange reserves
of industrialized countries totaled $87 billion. Of this
group only three countries--the United States, Japan, and
the Federal Republic of Germany--had reserves over $10
billion.

After very difficult experiences with defending par
values (supported in many areas with extensive foreign exchange controls) it is understandable that the flexible
exchange system was gradually adopted. Nevertheless, in
the context of current reform discussions, there are only
a few studies and/or suggestions as to how international
financial controls could be extended over multinational
corporations.


Other Organizations

It is ironic that other international organizations
have done more research and put forward more constructive
proposals concerning multinational corporations than GATT
and the IMF. The International Labor Organization (ILO)
and the International Bank for Reconstruction and Development (World Bank) are doing substantial research on multinationals. The ILO is interested chiefly in promoting fair
labor practices and the internationalization of labor
unions. The IBRD is doing major research to help understand the role of multinational corporations in economic
development in general, and in the transfer of technology
in particular. However, the most significant coordinated

effort in terms of developing international controls for multinationals is undertaken by the United Nations.[18] The "Group of Eminent Persons," appointed in 1973, explored almost every political and economic aspect of the increasing role of multinationals in the world economy. The final report of the Group, issued in the summer of 1974, includes 51 recommendations.[19] Perhaps the most important of these recommendations calls for a permanent 25-member commission on multinational corporations. The commission would be attached to the UN Economic and Social Council and would be supported by a new UN research agency on multinationals. In addition, the report also spelled out a set of procedures that host governments should follow in dealing with multinational corporations. For example, the Group emphasized that host governments should very clearly state in what sectors of their economy and under what specific conditions multinationals may invest and operate. It must be said that while all of the 51 recommendations appear reasonable and may represent a useful starting point, the problems of setting up an effective international mechanism that could eventually enforce the proposals of the planned commission and, consequently, could exert control over multinational corporations might be insurmountable.

## National Governments

Given the lack of international controls over multinational corporations, national governments are left to cope with the problem in their own ways. The national controls presently used vary from the regulation of transfer pricing practices to outright nationalization of property. It must be pointed out, however, that because many governments compete for investment by multinational corporations, most of the national control systems can be circumvented.

Multinational corporations provide numerous benefits to the host countries in which they set up operations. They provide employment, technology, and, through linkage, affect substantial growth in national income. On the other hand, through the circumvention of national controls, multinationals can also reduce or even eliminate most or all of these benefits.

To illustrate how the host country's benefits from multinationals may be diluted to the advantage of these corporations, a few examples are in order. The United States has negotiated over 20 bilateral tax agreements concerning withholding taxes on dividends and profits remitted to the United States. Under these agreements the withholding taxes (in addition to host country taxes on profits) may be as low as 5 percent versus 30 percent where no bilateral agreement exists. If a U.S.-based multinational has a subsidiary in a country with no bilateral agreement, the simple solution is to reincorporate the subsidiary in a country that has such an agreement. Thereby, the tax on remittances to the United States is reduced from 30 percent to 5 percent. Transfer pricing practices also provide good illustrations. For example, a high transfer price on imports enables multinationals to siphon off profit to a tax haven while reducing the profitability of the subsidiary subject to domestic taxes. This has two obvious effects: it increases the host country's balance-of-payments burden and reduces the government's revenues from the profit tax. This is done by multinational oil companies when pricing oil imports into the United States.[20]

National controls also have another interesting effect. Many countries attempt to control the international operations of their multinationals. In this regard the United States has received the most attention because of the relative number and size of U.S.-based multinational corporations. Under the U.S. Trading with the Enemy Act, U.S. citizens are forbidden to engage in commerce with certain nations. Insofar as U.S. nationals control the activities of subsidiaries in other countries, they are subject to the same law. In the past this has caused problems in trade with China, and, most of all, with Cuba. A locomotive sale to Cuba by a subsidiary of a U.S.-based multinational in Canada was blocked for several weeks under these provisions.[21] In April 1974, the American government permitted the Argentine subsidiaries of U.S.-based multinationals (General Motors, Ford, Chrysler) to sell cars and trucks to Cuba only after the Argentine government put severe pressure on the U.S. corporations. In both cases the U.S. multinationals involved found a simple solution; they replaced all U.S. citizens in the subsidiaries' top management with local nationals who could not be held responsible for the sale under U.S. law. While U.S. officials insist that both cases represent an exception granted on a one-time basis, it appears that in the future the nature and scope of such U.S. government controls will be reviewed and, eventually, changed. The U.S. government has also sought to block overseas mergers of U.S.-based multinationals for domestic antitrust reasons. The merger of Gillette and Braun in the Federal Republic of Germany, for example, was stopped as soon as it

became known to the U.S. government. While the extrater-
ritorial application of domestic policies and laws with
respect to multinationals based in a given country is a
problem leading to many conflicts, such conflicts are by
and large more of an irritant than a substantive matter of
great concern.

## IMPACT ON HOST COUNTRIES

Since multinational corporations have emerged as an
important international force, they have also been subjected to increasing criticism. In response to such criticism, spokesmen for the multinationals and for the countries that have substantially benefited from the presence
of these large corporations, have also become more vocal.
One of the major reasons that many countries want to attract multinationals includes the creation of new employment. Of all other advantages perhaps the most important
are training and technology transfer, which under certain
circumstances, via forward and backward linkages, can provide substantial benefits to host countries.

The major criticism of multinational corporations is
that they do not provide training of general usefulness
in the host economy and that they fail to shoulder a fair
share of the fiscal and balance-of-payments burdens. Multinational corporations, so the argument goes, seek low
cost labor and, consequently, provide chiefly manual jobs
requiring little or no skills. Moreover, as wages rise,
many multinationals simply divert some or all of their activities to another lower-wage economy. Initially, this
problem is created by the potential host countries who want
to attract the multinationals and is later on compounded
by the absence of effective international controls. There
are no easy solutions to this problem; actions by individual countries often result in countermeasures by multinational corporations leading to an undesirable reduction of
international investments.

## SUMMARY

Multinational corporations are not a new phenomenon.
The importance of modern multinationals is founded in
their autonomy, which arises from the lack of control over
their operations. Moreover, during the post-World War II
expansion of economic activity and the corresponding reduc-

tion in national restrictions, multinationals have grown even more rapidly than the nation states themselves. As a vehicle for international economic activity, they have surpassed the traditional channels of trade between nations. Their growth accompanied by the movement of factors of production, in particular of capital, across national boundaries has put heavy stress on the existing international agreements. Nevertheless, at present there are very few proposals to extend international controls over their activities.

Most countries engage in large-scale competition to attract multinational corporations because such corporations have become a vital link in the development of advanced-technology-based export industries. Multinationals, through their control over technology and distribution systems, have become an essential part of the industrialization process of developing economies. Nevertheless, as a result of the circumvention of national controls by multinationals, their contributions to industrialization have been less than expected. This problem can only be overcome by host country governments if they strictly control the conditions under which multinationals enter their economies. This has both positive and negative effects. It yields more benefits from the multinationals but reduces the attractiveness of the regulated economy, and may, therefore, lead to less than desired levels of foreign investment. At present, there is no easy solution to this dilemma.

The future of multinationals is promising. Their resourcefulness in the face of changing economic and financial conditions as well as regulatory legislation far exceeds that of domestically based operations. European and Japanese-based multinationals will probably expand at an increasing rate, thereby paralleling the growth of U.S.-based multinationals in the 1950-70 period. The main area of growth will probably come in manufacturing wherein multinationals will increasingly transfer labor-intensive operations to developing countries. It is, therefore, up to the developing countries to determine on what basis they will accept increased participation by multinationals. As a student of multinational corporations put it:

> Developing countries already subsidize multinational enterprises in many ways. Rather than moving toward repressive control measures, they should alter their incentive system in a positive way to bring about behavior they desire on the part of multinational enterprises.[22]

NOTES

1. See, for example, Miriam Beard, A History of Business (Ann Arbor, Mich.: Ann Arbor Paperback, 1962 reprint), vol. 1, pp. 11-14. For a broader perspective, see H. G. Wells, The Outline of History (New York: Garden City Books, 1961), pp. 127-65.

2. Beard, op. cit., p. 338.

3. For the early history of the Hudson's Bay Company, see E. F. Rich, Hudson's Bay Company 1670-1870 (Toronto: McClelland and Stewart, 1960).

4. Hudson's Bay Company, Annual Report, 1972.

5. Stefan H. Robuck and Kenneth Simonds, "International Business: How Big Is It? The Missing Measurements," Columbia Journal of World Business, May-June 1970, pp. 6-19.

6. United Nations, Multinational Corporations in World Development (ST/ECA/190), 1973, pp. 13-14. Given the sales estimates for subsidiaries of $330 billion in 1971, this estimate must make allowance for understatement as well as for the exclusion of sales by the headquarters company. It is not known if the authors adjusted the sales data to yield an estimate of value added.

7. Ibid., pp. 10-11.

8. Louis Turner, Multinational Corporations and the Third World (New York: Hill and Wang, 1973), pp. 175-209.

9. Frank Mastrapasqua, U.S. Expansion via Foreign Branching: Monetary Policy Implications (New York: New York University Press, 1973), pp. 23-25.

10. Ralph M. Gaedeke, "Selected U.S. Multinational Service Firms in Perspective," Journal of International Business Studies (Spring 1973).

11. Stephen Hymer, "The International Operations of National Firms, A Study of Direct Investment," unpublished Ph.D. dissertation, Massachusetts Institute of Technology (1960).

12. See, for example, H. G. Johnson, "The Efficiency and Welfare Implications of International Corporations," in The International Corporation, ed. C. P. Kindleberger (Boston: Massachusetts Institute of Technology Press, 1970); and R. E. Caves, "International Corporations: The Industrial Economics of Foreign Investment," Economica, February 1971, pp. 1403-17.

13. J. H. Dunning, The Multinational Enterprise (London: Allen and Unwin, 1971).

14. GATT Information (GATT/1133), September 1973.

15. GATT Activities in 1972, Geneva, 1973.

16.  Sidney Gott, The GATT Negotiations, 1973-75:  A Guide to the Issues (Montreal:  British North American Committee, April 1974), p. 57.

17.  U.S. Senate, Committee on Finance, The Multinational Corporations and the World Economy (Washington, D.C.:  U.S. Government Printing Office, 1973), p. 30.

18.  The UN Economic and Social Council, Resolution 1721 (LIII) adopted unanimously July 28, 1972 requested the Secretary-General to appoint a "Group of Eminent Persons" to study MNCs, particularly with respect to their role in development.

19.  UN Economic and Social Council, The Impact of Multinational Corporations on the Development Process and on International Relations (E/5500), June 12, 1974.

20.  U.S. Senate hearings on Multinational Corporations (1974), presented evidence with respect to Armaco's transfer pricing policies.  See Washington Post, March 28, 1974, p. 14.

21.  MLW-Worthington Lts. of Montreal, a subsidiary of Studebaker-Worthington, Inc., New York, was seeking to export $15 million of locomotives and spare parts to Cuba. The sale was reportedly completed.  Wall Street Journal, March 19, 1974, p. 14.

22.  R. Hal Mason, "The Multinational Firm and the Cost of Technology to Developing Countries," California Management Review, Summer 1973, p. 13.

# 2

## THE EASTERN EUROPEAN
## SOCIALIST ECONOMIES

Following the United States (28.2 percent), Western Europe (25.2 percent), the Soviet Union (14.5 percent), and Japan (7.3 percent), Bulgaria, Czechoslovakia, the German Democratic Republic, Hungary, Poland, and Romania claimed the fifth largest share (5.5 percent) of total world economic output for 1972.[1] In terms of 1972 economic performance, the Eastern European socialist economies were ahead of Latin America, the Far East (excluding Japan), Africa, and the Middle East. Table 2.1 provides a breakdown of additional demographic and economic data for the region.

Thus, with a total population of approximately 104 million people, an average economic growth rate of about 5 percent for the 1967-72 period, and a median per capita income of U.S. $1,296 in 1972, the Eastern European socialist economies have emerged as an important economic group.[2] Table 2.2 presents data showing their world trade involvement in 1972.

Table 2.3 provides data concerning the trade involvement of the Eastern European socialist economies with the industrialized Western world in 1972.

Table 2.4 shows a detailed breakdown of the development of this trade over time.

The trade involvement of the Eastern European socialist economies with the industrialized Western world grew rapidly during the 1969-72 period. This growth, together with more trade with the rest of the world, increased their share in total 1972 world trade to about $36 billion or 12 percent. It should be noted, however, that at the same time the share of the socialist economies in total world industrial output stood at 33 percent. Moreover, 60 per-

TABLE 2.1

Eastern European Socialist Economies: Demographic and Economic Data, 1972

| Country | Population | | | GNP[a] | | National Income | | |
|---|---|---|---|---|---|---|---|---|
| | Total, 1972 (million $) | Percent Increase, Past Five Years | UN Forecast, 1980 | Total, 1972 (billion $) | Percent Five-Year Increase, Constant Prices | Total, 1972 (billion $) | Percent Five-Year Increase, Current Prices | Per Capita, 1972 (dollars) |
| Bulgaria | 8.6 | 3.2 | 9.2 | 13.5[b] | 42.1 | 6.1[c] | 44.5 | 741 |
| Czechoslovakia | 14.5 | 1.2 | 15.8 | 35.2[b] | 19.3 | 21.1[c] | 46.7 | 1,455 |
| German Democratic Republic | 17.0 | -0.2 | 17.7 | 43.3[b] | 23.7 | 37.5[c] | 29.1 | 2,208 |
| Hungary | 10.4 | 1.9 | 10.8 | 17.2[b] | 18.4 | 11.5[c] | 53.7 | 1,110 |
| Poland | 33.1 | 3.5 | 36.6 | 52.0[b] | 26.8 | 42.9[c] | 56.4 | 1,296 |
| Romania | 20.8 | 7.7 | 22.4 | 28.8[b] | 37.8 | 11.8[d] | n.a. | 570[d] |

[a]Gross social product as defined by the Socialist countries.

[b]In constant 1970 dollars.

[c]Net material product.

[d]National income estimated as 0.41 of GNP in constant prices. There are no price statistics available; consumer prices are administered and during the period 1968-72 they were adjusted only marginally and infrequently resulting in overall price increases of probably less than 2 percent.

Source: Business International, December 7, 1973, p. 390.

TABLE 2.2

World Trade Involvement of Socialist Economies, 1972
(billions of dollars)

| Country | National Income | Exports | Exports as Percent of National Income |
|---|---|---|---|
| Bulgaria | 6.1 | 2.6 | 42.6 |
| Czechoslovakia | 21.2 | 5.1 | 24.0 |
| German Democratic Republic | 37.5 | 6.1 | 16.2 |
| Hungary | 11.5 | 3.2 | 27.8 |
| Poland | 42.9 | 4.9 | 11.4 |
| Romania | 11.8 | 2.9 | 24.6 |

Sources: Computed from Business International, December 7, 1973, p. 390, except for Romania. Export data for Romania from Anuarul Statistic al Republicii Socialiste Romania, 1973, p. 467.


TABLE 2.3

Trade Involvement of Socialist Economies with the West, 1972
(billions of dollars)

| Country | National Income | Exports | Exports as Percent of National Income |
|---|---|---|---|
| Bulgaria | 6.1 | 0.32 | 5.2 |
| Czechoslovakia | 21.2 | 1.05 | 4.9 |
| German Democratic Republic | 37.5 | 1.17 | 3.1 |
| Hungary | 11.5 | 0.75 | 6.5 |
| Poland | 42.9 | 1.45 | 3.3 |
| Romania | 11.8 | 0.82 | 6.9 |

Sources: Computed from Business International Eastern Europe Report, 1973 issues; and from Anuarul Statistic al Republicii Socialiste Romania, 1973, p. 467.

TABLE 2.4

Development of Eastern European Trade with Western Industrial Countries
(millions of current dollars)

| | 1960 | 1970 | Percent Increase 1969-70 | 1971 | Percent Increase 1970-71 | 1972 | Percent Increase 1971-72 |
|---|---|---|---|---|---|---|---|
| Exports[a] | | | | | | | |
| Bulgaria | 73.8 | 284.7 | 9.7 | 306.1 | 7.5 | 320.0 | 4.5 |
| Czechoslovakia | 330.9 | 778.1 | 9.2 | 851.7 | 9.5 | 1,053.8 | 23.7 |
| German Democratic Re-public | 424.8 | 903.4 | 23.6 | 954.7 | 5.7 | 1,177.7 | 23.4 |
| Hungary | 197.0 | 657.3 | 21.6 | 574.4 | -12.6 | 755.0 | 31.4 |
| Poland | 386.2 | 1,011.4 | 19.2 | 1,147.8 | 13.5 | 1,453.8 | 26.7 |
| Romania | 153.0 | 596.9 | 20.2 | 714.7 | 19.7 | 820.0 | 14.7 |
| Total | 1,565.7 | 4,231.8 | 17.9 | 4,549.4 | 7.5 | 5,580.3 | 22.7 |
| Imports[b] | | | | | | | |
| Bulgaria | 88.9 | 350.6 | 36.6 | 360.1 | 2.7 | 360.1 | 0.0 |
| Czechoslovakia | 356.5 | 912.7 | 25.6 | 1,001.1 | 9.7 | 1,083.8 | 8.3 |
| German Democratic Re-public | 451.6 | 1,082.4 | 26.9 | 1,217.2 | 12.5 | 1,542.4 | 26.7 |
| Hungary | 250.2 | 741.2 | 42.6 | 826.6 | 11.5 | 883.0 | 6.8 |
| Poland | 445.8 | 933.4 | 4.2 | 1,110.7 | 19.0 | 1,790.4 | 61.2 |
| Romania | 152.2 | 776.3 | 5.1 | 835.3 | 7.6 | 983.0 | 17.7 |
| Total | 1,745.0 | 4,796.6 | 20.2 | 5,351.0 | 11.5 | 6,642.7 | 24.1 |

[a] f.o.b.
[b] c.i.f.

Source: Business International Eastern Europe Report, December 28, 1973, pp. 380-81.

cent, or about $21.6 billion of their total world trade
share represented trade within the framework of the Council
for Mutual Economic Assistance (CMEA), which is the socialist world's economic organization (founded in 1949) to improve trade and to promote economic growth throughout the
Eastern European region.

East-West trade is asymmetrical.[3] Well over half of
Western exports to Eastern Europe consist of manufactured
goods while only less than half of the socialist exports
to the West are in the same category. Eastern European
exports are, among others, negatively affected by the relatively inefficient industrial structures, the inflexible
nature of planned foreign trade, balance-of-payments difficulties, price competition among CMEA members in hard
currency markets, bilateral trade agreements with Western
countries that make imports conditional on the equivalent
purchase of goods by Western partners, and, finally, by
the relatively low quality of many manufactured goods and
unsophisticated marketing approaches.

Some recent developments indicate that in the long
run these problems might be gradually eliminated. The UN
Economic Commission for Europe reported in 1973 that over
the 1952-72 period Eastern European output structures
changed more than Western European ones. The report also
pointed out that output structures and foreign trade patterns of both regions are becoming more similar in that the
share of manufactured goods in Eastern European exports is
slowly increasing.[4] Finally, the Eastern European socialist economies are trying to work out a procedure through
which they can eliminate price competition with each other
in hard currency markets.

OUTLOOK FOR THE 1970s

The overall outlook for the 1970s indicates continued
domestic development throughout the region. Total population is expected to reach 113 million by 1980.[5] The average annual economic growth rate is forecast to be in the
neighborhood of 5 percent. Average industrial output is
estimated to increase between 7.3 and 7.9 percent annually;
this would raise the share of the Eastern European socialist economies in total world industrial output to 36 percent by 1980.[6] This compares favorably with a 16.6 percent share in 1950, and a 30.5 percent share in 1968.[7]
Table 2.5 presents average annual growth rates in the
various sectors for the 1971-75 period as projected (quite

TABLE 2.5

Average Annual Growth Rates for Various Sectors, 1971-75 Economic Plans
(percent)

| | Bulgaria | Czecho-slovakia | German Democratic Republic | Hungary | Poland | Romania |
|---|---|---|---|---|---|---|
| Consumption | 8.5 | 5.0-5.4 | 3.9-4.2 | 5.5 | 6.7 | 7.6 |
| Fixed investment | 6.4 | 6.0-6.5 | 5.0-5.4 | 5.5 | 6.7 | 10.4 |
| Industrial production | 9-10 | 6.0-6.4 | 6.0 | 6.0-6.5 | 8.2-8.4 | 11-12.3 |
| Producer goods | -- | -- | -- | -- | 8.6 | -- |
| Consumer goods | 8.5 | -- | 3.9-4.2 | 10-11 | 7.3 | -- |
| Electric power | 9.0 | 6.8 | 5.4-5.9 | -- | 8.3 | 9.5-10.5 |
| Iron and steel | -- | -- | 6.5-7.0 | -- | -- | 9.5-10.0 |
| Engineering | 17.0 | 7.5 | 8.2 | -- | 10.9 | 17 |
| Chemicals | -- | 10.0 | 8.0 | -- | -- | 18 |
| Light industry | -- | 4.6 | 5.7 | -- | 9.6 | -- |
| Food industry | -- | 3.4 | 3.4 | -- | -- | -- |
| Industrial productivity | 7.6 | 5.4-5.7 | 6.1-6.5 | 4.1-4.4 | 5.6-5.9 | 7.3 |
| Agricultural production | 3.2-3.7 | 2.7 | 2.4 | 2.8-3.1 | 3.5-3.9 | 6.3-8.3 |
| Construction | -- | 6.7 | 5.0-5.3 | 7.0-7.5 | -- | -- |

Source: Thomas A. Wolf, "New Frontiers in East-West Trade," European Business, Autumn 1973, p. 33.

optimistically in some cases) in the individual country plans.

The development plans of all socialist countries are predicated on a switch from extensive to intensive economic growth. This change from promoting growth through the addition of new plants and increases in the labor force to promoting growth through a more efficient utilization of existing plants and labor was the result of widespread industrial inefficiency that became too costly. It was also caused by the gradually emerging labor shortages. To more efficiently use existing resources, the socialist economies have to adopt advanced technology; they must replace old equipment, modernize production processes, and update management know-how.

To do all of these things the Eastern Europeans need hard currency. Foreign trade projections for the traditional channels of trade, until 1980, however, are not very optimistic. Although the average annual growth is expected to be 8.7 percent for exports and 9.1 percent for imports, forecasters do not expect the Eastern European socialist economies to substantially increase their share (about $36 billion, or 12 percent in 1972) of total world trade.[8] Moreover, as approximately 60 percent of this total world-trade share represents trade within the framework of CMEA, it is clear that through the traditional means of foreign trade the socialist economies cannot generate enough hard currency to obtain the needed products, technology, and know-how. Consequently, the Eastern European countries have to develop new kinds of economic ties to the Western world in general, and to the dominating Western economic institutions, the multinational corporations, in particular.

## ECONOMIC AND MANAGERIAL STRUCTURES

The change from extensive to intensive growth began with a set of economic reforms during the 1960s. The scope of these reforms varies from country to country.[9] Hungary's New Economic Mechanism, for example, was based on a restructuring of the entire economic system in 1968.[10] In contrast, reforms in Bulgaria, Czechoslovakia, the German Democratic Republic, Poland, and Romania tend to be far more limited. Regardless of the scope of the reforms, however, the changes in every country were introduced on an ideological basis--the central authorities emphasized that the supreme guiding role of Marxism-Leninism in all aspects of life would not be reduced by the economic reforms.

The objectives of the reforms were generally defined
as the elimination of the rigid and wearisome features of
past economic systems, the establishment of the superiority
of Marxism-Leninism over the capitalist system, the introduction of "objective economic laws," and the promotion of
continued economic development.[11] Within the framework of
the strict ideological guidelines and the stated objectives,
the reforms led to the adoption of numerous economic concepts ("objective economic laws") long known and applied
in the capitalist world. This, in turn, resulted in changes
in the role of central planning and led to the limited
utilization of the marketplace, competition, and profits.

In general, central planning in most countries has become less comprehensive and the meeting of the plan targets
by individual enterprises has become less compulsory. However, only in Hungary did the reformers draw the necessary
conclusions from past experience. As of 1968, the central
authorities in Hungary no longer develop compulsory plans
for enterprises, and enterprise performance is instead
measured chiefly through profits earned in the marketplace.
In most other countries, centrally guided enterprise plans
are still used as standards of performance and the measur-
ing concept, in addition to profit, is the "100 percent
fulfillment of realistically demanding enterprise plans"
that are realized through "the maximum exploitation of opportunities."

In all the reformed economies the marketplace plays
an increasingly important role, although only in Hungary
does it serve as a meeting place for buyers and sellers
who are free to choose their trading partners. In the
other countries, there are still limits on the trading activities of the various industrial and commercial enterprises. In some cases, compulsory channels of distribution and in others, compulsory trading contracts limit the
free flow of goods. Under such conditions, the nature and
limits of competition are defined by the special characteristics of the reformed marketplaces, which not only perform
a limited regulatory function but also are themselves regulated. For example, in every country the central authorities still plan and determine the aggregate purchasing
power of the population, oversee or set prices, allocate
foreign exchange for imports, and, if necessary, redefine
enterprise activities.

The introduction of some aspects of the marketplace
and limited competition resulted in every reformed economy
in the acceptance of profit as one of the most important
enterprise success indicators. There are, however, certain

limitations on the use of profit to judge enterprise per-
formance--for example, the widespread sellers' market conditions, the various restrictions on competition, continued
regulation of prices, and the granting of enterprise subsidies.  In Hungary, for example, a November 1972 government directive instructed economic policy makers to "pay
special attention to the activities and problems of the
40-50 largest industrial enterprises in the country and to
support the same every way whenever necessary."[12]  Since
such large enterprises include numerous smaller ones, the
total number of enterprises receiving "special attention"
during the 1971-75 plan period amounts to approximately
180.  As such they represent a significant part of the Hungarian economy.  Nevertheless, the reformers in Hungary
and every other socialist country believe that together
with less tangible but not less important standards--such
as the rate of technical invention and social contribution--
profit is still one of the best comprehensive indicators
of enterprise performance.

Within the reformed economies in every country a considerable amount of economic decision-making authority has
been decentralized to the enterprise level.  To varying degrees, managers have authority to make or to delegate independent decisions in the areas of enterprise planning,
hiring, promotion and transfer of employees, technological
developments, product policies, enterprise organizational
structures, and enterprise operating procedures.  In Hungary managers even have the authority to make independent
investment decisions, establish credit and some price policies, and to form enterprise associations as well as to
lease unneeded equipment.  Naturally, decisions in all of
the above-mentioned areas have to be made in every country
within the existing legal framework and in line with the
economic policy guidelines issued by the central authorities.

To enable enterprise managers to make or to delegate
independent decisions in the above-mentioned areas, changes
were also made in the supply systems, the price systems,
investment and credit systems, in the area of labor relations, work incentives, foreign trade, and management education and development.  In general, all such changes were
designated to insure that the increased managerial independence could be exercised without any unnecessary interfer-
ence from the central authorities.

Despite the greatly increased managerial independence,
the Central Committees of the Parties and the Council of
Ministers continue as the supreme authorities.  The leading

30

role of the parties in the political, economic, social, and cultural life of the different countries has not been reduced by the reforms. Great care is taken by the central authorities everywhere that this should not happen.

Operating on the basis of the directives issued by the Central Committees and Council of Ministers, the central authorities continue as the immediate overseers of economic activities. They are responsible for the development and effective administration of the various industrial branches according to the national plans, and their supervisory authority includes the power to start new enterprises, to redefine enterprise activities, to appoint and dismiss top enterprise managers, to evaluate and audit enterprise performance, and, if in the national interest, to issue specific operational instructions to enterprise managers.

As pointed out before, while the objectives and the general nature of the reforms are quite similar in every country, the technical details of implementation and day-to-day management tend to differ. There are several reasons for such differences. First, the various sizes of the countries--reform measures that are easily applicable in small economies cannot necessarily be used the same way in larger economies and vice versa. Second, the varying levels of economic development--Czechoslovakia, for example, is more developed than Bulgaria, and consequently the Czechs have different economic needs and opportunities. Third, the degree of dependence on foreign trade--countries that depend heavily on foreign trade for their development as, for example, Hungary, which generates about 40 percent of its national income from the foreign trade sector, have to take this into account in developing, implementing, and managing the reform. Finally, historically conditioned differences in terms of national temperament and outlook. Economic reforms have to be implemented and managed by people whose attitudes toward life in general and work in particular can no longer be entirely ignored by the various socialist governments.

## THE COUNCIL FOR MUTUAL
## ECONOMIC ASSISTANCE

As mentioned previously, about 60 percent of the total foreign trade volume of the Eastern European socialist economies represents trade within the framework of the Council for Mutual Economic Assistance (CMEA).[13] Table 2.6 presents data concerning the trend and distribution of intra-CMEA trade over time. As can be seen from these data, Romania substantially decreased both its share of exports and imports over the last few years. The German Democratic Republic, Poland, and Hungary increased exports to, but decreased imports from, the other CMEA countries. Only Bulgaria, the least developed member, increased both its exports and imports. These developments indicate heavier reliance of the majority on trade with the West.

About 70 percent of intra-CMEA trade is transacted under long-term bilateral trade agreements in which the price of goods exchanged is usually fixed for five or more years.[14] In working out the agreements, the trading partners attempt to balance their exports and imports--that is, imports are determined not only by cost comparisons but also by the ability to market exports in the partner country. As a result, both the efficiency of production and the volume of trade are reduced and the desired international (socialist) division of labor is impaired.

Furthermore, domestic price systems do not reflect true economic costs, and in most countries deviations between domestic and foreign prices continue to be significant. Frequently, foreign trade prices are applicable only to trade with a particular country. The "transfer ruble,"

TABLE 2.6

Trend and Distribution of Intra-CMEA Trade
(as a percentage of total trade)

| Country | Exports | | | | Imports | | | |
|---|---|---|---|---|---|---|---|---|
| | 1960 | 1970 | 1971 | 1972 | 1960 | 1970 | 1971 | 1972 |
| Bulgaria | 80.4 | 75.5 | 75.6 | 77.7 | 79.5 | 72.6 | 74.0 | 76.7 |
| Czechoslovakia | 63.5 | 64.3 | 63.8 | 63.9 | 63.9 | 63.2 | 63.6 | 65.1 |
| German Democratic Republic | 68.7 | 68.5 | 69.1 | 70.1 | 70.9 | 66.0 | 65.0 | 62.8 |
| Hungary | 61.3 | 61.2 | 64.9 | 65.5 | 63.6 | 61.7 | 63.0 | 62.7 |
| Poland | 54.9 | 60.2 | 59.2 | 60.3 | 58.1 | 65.5 | 63.9 | 57.9 |
| Romania | 65.6 | 50.1 | 47.8 | 46.8 | 67.8 | 48.2 | 46.1 | 43.8 |

Source: Business International Eastern Europe Report, December 28, 1973, pp. 380-81.

introduced as a first approximation of a common currency
in 1964, has not yet fulfilled expectations. For the transfer ruble to be an effective medium of exchange, it would
have to be the common denominator of production costs and
national currencies convertible regionally at their approx-
imate purchasing power. Such conditions, however, still
do not exist, consequently, multilateral trade and integra-
tion--that is, an effective international division of labor
and economic cooperation between the member countries--is
still not feasible.

Intra-CMEA trade is characterized by artificially high
export prices for manufactured goods. This is the result
of widespread sellers' market conditions and bilateral
trade agreements that induce countries to charge higher
export prices whenever they have to pay high import prices.
Differing cost measurement methods and, consequently, price
setting procedures add to the problem. During the early
1960s, for example, the intra-CMEA price level was approximately 20 percent higher than the world-market price level;
during the late 1960s the difference was reduced to about
10 percent.[15] Due to the substantial increase in oil and
other raw material world prices during 1973/74, this difference, at least for the time being, is probably further
reduced because most Eastern European socialist economies
import their oil and raw materials from the Soviet Union
under long-term price contracts. (The current contracts
expire at the end of 1975.) Nevertheless, the general
intra-CMEA trade price level is probably still higher than
the general world-market price level.

Another important characteristic of intra-CMEA trade
is the dominant position of the Soviet Union. Table 2.7
presents data concerning the past and projected shares of
the socialist economies in Soviet foreign trade.

As can be seen from these data, Soviet trade with the
CMEA countries is projected to increase during 1971-75.
At the same time, it should be noted that the volume of
Soviet trade with individual countries is changing. The
most dramatic changes are the 2.6 percent increase for the
German Democratic Republic and the 0.1 percent projected
decrease for Romania.

Despite the continuous increase in total trade between the Soviet Union and the other CMEA countries, it is
important to remember that in the long run the Soviet
Union is also interested in increasing trade with the West
and that some of the current CMEA trading practices are
contrary to Soviet national interests. Under current practices, all CMEA countries, except Romania, obtain most of

TABLE 2.7

Past and Projected CMEA Member Shares in Soviet
Foreign Trade
(in percentages)

| Country | Share in Soviet Foreign Trade | | Increase, |
| | 1966-70 | 1971-75 | Decrease |
| --- | --- | --- | --- |
| Bulgaria | 8.5 | 10.1 | 1.6 |
| Czechoslovakia | 10.3 | 11.0 | 0.7 |
| German Democratic Republic | 15.3 | 17.9 | 2.6 |
| Hungary | 6.6 | 7.5 | 0.9 |
| Poland | 10.2 | 10.6 | 0.4 |
| Romania | 4.4 | 4.3 | (0.1) |

Source: Kozgazdasagi Szemle (Economic Review), July-August 1973, p. 947.

the needed raw materials from the Soviet Union at less than world-market prices. Furthermore, CMEA countries sell most of their industrial output of less than world-market quality in the Soviet Union. Thus, the Soviets are absorbing otherwise unsalable products.

It now appears that such arrangements are less and less acceptable to the Soviet Union. During the June 1973 CMEA meeting in Prague, the Soviet representative observed that there are limits to the raw material deliveries of the Soviet Union, especially if the other CMEA countries continue to purchase most of their machines and equipment either in Western markets or from each other, but not from the Soviet Union.[16] Furthermore, he emphasized that CMEA countries in general, and Czechoslovakia in particular, must improve the quality of products delivered to the Soviet Union. In the future many such products have to include imported materials and have to be manufactured under Western licensing. Finally, during a regular 1974 CMEA meeting the Soviet representative also informed the other countries that because of world oil-market developments (price increases to $8-10 a barrel), the Soviet Union will not be able to maintain the $2-a-barrel oil price beyond the 1975 expiration date of the current long-term contracts.

Other CMEA countries also complain. The Hungarians, for example, are dissatisfied with the large export surpluses they have built up with other CMEA countries in 1973 and afterward. Many CMEA consumer products imported by Hungary cannot be sold; Hungarian consumers are too sophisticated and demanding. As the clearing credits (transfer rubles) earned in one socialist country cannot be spent in another, and as the quality of CMEA products does not improve fast enough, the Hungarians view such problems with great misgivings. As Poland and Czechoslovakia have experienced similar problems and expressed similar views, it is probably reasonable to say that in terms of member country expectations and demands, intra-CMEA trade is about to enter a new era. The 1974 changes in the intra-CMEA clearing process, whereby mutual trade accounts are to be balanced every three years and not annually, may be indicative of impending developments. How soon and how effectively such expectations and demands can be translated into new trading arrangements is, of course, another question.

To help overcome intra-CMEA problems a 15-to-20-year "Complex Program" was accepted at the 25th CMEA meeting in Bucharest, Romania, in July 1971. The major long-range objective of the program is economic integration. More specifically: to increase economic growth and living standards, to create a higher degree of self-sufficiency for the community, to strengthen defense postures, and to improve intra-CMEA trade. To accomplish the last objective, the socialist countries want to create economic conditions that would enable member countries to produce goods in whose production they have comparative advantages and economies of scale. Accordingly, the "Complex Program" calls for a great number of consultative meetings and a coordination of national plans in terms of specific details, such as investment, research and development, and financial aims. The program also specifies the creation of various committees, such as the Committee for Planning and Coordination and the Committee for Scientific and Technical Cooperation. One of the responsibilities of the latter committee, for example, is the development of a common set of performance and product quality standards for industries that are to be integrated.

Although one of the objectives of the "Complex Program" is the improvement of intra-CMEA trade, no significant changes are currently taking place in the trading system. National plans and bilateral agreements continue to serve as a basis for trade, although the use of quotas might be somewhat reduced over the coming years. Furthermore, there is a possibility of all CMEA countries developing a joint export pricing schedule for trade with the West so as to avoid competing with each other in hard currency markets. This should lessen intra-CMEA trade tensions, and together with the detailed price studies undertaken, might pave the way to 1980 when decisions concerning realistic exchange rates and the role of the transfer ruble have to be reached.

On the whole, the "Complex Program" appears to represent a set of generally accepted theoretical guidelines for the future development of the region. The problems of applying the guidelines to practical situations, however, seem to be formidable. Students of CMEA have pointed out, for example, that differences in levels of economic development, nature of economic reforms, degree of dependence on foreign trade, and related issues are bound to create misunderstandings (different expectations and demands) among the member countries.[17] They have argued that the guidelines accepted in Bucharest were agreed to at the level of the lowest common denominator and, consequently, tend to be vague and, at times, even contradictory. It was also pointed out that CMEA integration could very easily perpetuate inefficient intra-CMEA trade patterns.

It is, of course, much too early to determine the success or failure of the integration effort. While the problems generated by the different expectations and demands are difficult to overcome, some of the recent developments are promising. Since the acceptance of the "Complex Program" in 1971, for example, more than 60 multilateral agreements were signed; 11 of these deal with specialization of production, and 41 with scientific-technical cooperation.[18] One of the production specialization agreements covers the heavy truck manufacturing industries of the Soviet Union, Romania, and Czechoslovakia. Another deals with the light truck building industries of Poland, Bulgaria, Czechoslovakia, and Hungary. In June 1972, the first CMEA equity joint venture also got under way. The German Democratic Republic and Poland agreed to build a cotton fiber plant in Poland, each owning 50 percent of the venture. The general manager is Polish, his deputy German, and the remaining top managerial positions are equally divided. Investments, cost of operation, and earnings are also equally shared. In 1973, a multi-CMEA venture was signed in Moscow. The agreement calls for the joint construction, equipment, and operation of a cellulose combine in the Soviet Union. It has to be pointed out, however, that the production specialization agreements have a major weakness: in the majority of cases they are based on end-product specialization. This is not in harmony with the production specialization developments in the rest of the world where the end products are assembled in special plants from intermediary units and parts produced by also highly specialized plants. One of the major reasons for this CMEA problem is that trade agreements are made at the governmental level and that the execution of trade agreements is done by foreign trade and not by manufacturing enterprises. The high level trade agreements are not based on a detailed analysis of manufacturing conditions and market demand. Further, the involvement of foreign trade enterprises makes direct communication between manufacturing plants very difficult.

Nevertheless, to facilitate the agreements, 3,459 industrial standardization agreements were adopted by the end of 1971; 3,137 of these in manufacturing with about 55 percent in engineering products, 20 percent in metal products, 17 percent in chemicals and oil products, and the rest in other kinds of manufactured goods.[19] Business International reported in 1973 that continued progress is made by the CMEA member countries toward the adoption of "common standards of measurement, performance and quality for industries that will be integrated under the COMECON Complex Program."[20]

The International Bank for Economic Cooperation (IBEC), founded in 1964, and the International Investment Bank (IIB), set up in 1971, have also aligned their policies with the "Complex Program" objectives. While the continued use of bilateral agreements in intra-CMEA trade limits the trade financing activities of IBEC, IIB has been quite active during the past years. In 1972, for example, 33 percent of the total credit granted was given to the vehicle manufacturing industries of several countries: about 25 percent to the machine building, 24 percent to the chemical, and 11 percent to the light industries.[21] All these industries are targets of early CMEA integration efforts.

## RELATIONSHIP TO THE INTERNATIONAL
## TRADE AND PAYMENT SYSTEM

With the recognition that increased trade with the West is necessary for intensive growth, the relations of the Eastern European socialist economies to the international trade and payment system have multiplied. Czechoslovakia was one of the founding members of the General Agreement on Tariffs and Trade (GATT), Poland joined in 1967, and Romania in 1971. Hungary also became a member in 1973, thus, for the time being, only Bulgaria and the

German Democratic Republic remain outside this important international organization for multilateral trade negotiations. Both Bulgaria and the German Democratic Republic will eventually apply for membership. Consequently, the day when East-West trade will no longer be hampered by major discriminatory practices might not be too far off.

Despite continuous balance-of-payment and development financing problems, Eastern European membership in the International Monetary Fund (IMF), and the International Bank for Reconstruction and Development (World Bank), is far more limited. Since Romania joined both institutions in 1972, approximately 25 percent of its hard currency earnings are spent on interest and principal of hard currency credits that are needed to finance its development plans; it draws on its gold tranche the equivalent of 25 percent of its quota, or SDR 47.5 million in May 1973.[22] To underline its commitment to the international trade and payments system, the Romanian government has announced that it plans to make its currency, the lei, convertible in the future. While no specific date has yet been set for such a move, the announcement put Romania in a unique position in socialist Eastern Europe.

Eastern European contacts and deals with Western capital markets have increased considerably during the last few years. In 1971, Hungary became the first Eastern European socialist country to offer a $20 million bond issue, underwritten by leading Western financial institutions, in Western European capital markets. This first issue was followed by a $50 million offering underwritten, among others, by the Bank of America and the Japanese International Bank. Most of the other socialist countries, however, are more reluctant to raise capital in the West through bond issues. They consider the interest rates too high and, consequently, tend to obtain the lower interest rate suppliers' loans that Western export credit and insurance institutions provide. The CMEA International Investment Bank is, like Hungary, less conservative; in 1973 it obtained a $50 million, seven-year loan from a syndicate headed by the National Westminister Bank of England.

To help finance Western trade, several socialist banks have set up joint operations in the West. In 1973 the Romanian Foreign Trade Bank, for example, set up a joint bank with Manufacturers Hanover Trust and the Barclay Bank of London. The same year the Polish Trade Bank and the West German Hessische Landesbank Girozentrale opened their joint institution in Frankfurt, West Germany. In 1973, Hungary opened a bank, the Hungarian International Bank

Ltd., in London, England.  About 60 percent of the bank's
capital of £1 million is owned by the Hungarian National
Bank, 15 percent each by the Hungarian Foreign Trade and
National Savings Banks.  The remaining 10 percent was sub-
scribed to by the Central Wechsel and Credit Bank of Vienna,
Austria, also a Hungarian-owned financial institution.  Finally, it is also worth mentioning that in 1974 a major
Western bank opened its first branch office in socialist
Eastern Europe.  On the invitation of the Romanian government, Manufacturers Hanover of the United States started
banking operations in Bucharest.  Staffed by both U.S. and
Romanian nationals, the bank serves as a base for financing
and promoting East-West trade.

## CHANGING VIEWS ON MULTINATIONAL
## CORPORATIONS

Although multinational corporations are not a new
phenomenon, it was only a few years ago that they were
recognized in the Western world as important economic organizations that, for better or worse, have the potential
to change future international relations in general, and
trade patterns in particular.  Since this recognition, the
Western world has been flooded by a great variety of published material--supportive and critical--dealing with almost every possible past, present, and future aspect of
multinational corporations.

Comprehensive and analytical Eastern European views
on multinationals are even more recent.  This is understandable because prior to the switch from extensive to
intensive economic growth and the emerging détente there
was no need to recognize them except in the briefest and
most ideological terms.  Accordingly, pre-1969-70, Eastern
European publications dealing with multinationals were
limited mostly to extremely critical magazine and newspaper articles.  The authors generally described multinational corporations as business organizations that were
developed for the sole purpose of furthering the imperialist aims of Western--especially American--capitalists the
world over.  As most of these articles were based on critical reports first published in the West and were authored
by political journalists, they lacked both originality and
analytical quality.

With the switch from extensive to intensive economic
growth, and the resulting increased demand for advanced
Western technology, products, and know-how, the Eastern

European socialist countries gradually revised their views
on multinational corporations. Government officials and
academicians began to pay close attention to the role multinationals are playing in the world economy. Moreover,
as a result of the détente, exchange of information between
East and West became less restricted and thus researchers
on both sides began exploring issues of mutual interest.
As could be expected, all of this resulted in less rigid
and more analytical views on multinational corporations--
first in those socialist countries that depend heavily on
international trade and where the economic reforms of the
late 1960s and early 1970s were the most far-reaching.

Consequently, the first comprehensive and analytical
study of multinational corporations was published in Hungary in 1970. America in Europe: Corporate Empires in
the World Economy, by Gyorgy Adam, is a massive book of
about 500 pages exploring, as the author stated in his
preface, "the emerging relationship between the expansion
of U.S. business in Western Europe and the multinational
corporation."[23] Adam argues that the first development,
the expansion of U.S. business in Western Europe, led to
the second one, the emergence of multinational corporations
as major factors in the world economy. To support his contention, he marshals an impressive array of economic data
published by a variety of Western governmental and private
organizations. He also relies on the classics of Marxism,
such as V. I. Lenin's Imperialism as the Highest Form of
Capitalism, and on the early works of such acknowledged
Western experts on multinational corporations as Behrman,
Dunning, Kindleberger, Perlmutter, and Vernon.

Adam's book, as could be expected, is critical but
his negative views are generally within the acceptable
limits of scholarly analysis and are not distorted by rigid
ideological arguments. His approach is that of a scholarly
Marxist critic who knows Western political and economic
developments, who is aware of the relevant literature and
who, on his own terms, wants to understand and not just
criticize multinational corporations. Although he discusses the emergence of Western European multinationals,
he sees the spreading political, economic, and social power
of large corporations as chiefly an American phenomenon, a
view that was justified when he completed his research
during the late 1960s. (The Fortune listings of May and
September 1973, pp. 220-47, and pp. 202-03, show that this
view is no longer entirely justified.) In addition to
criticizing the vast negative potential of multinationals,
Adam, however, also points out the positive role these

large corporations play in the international transfer of technology and management know-how. As Adam's previous research dealt with research and development and technology transfer, he presents a very knowledgeable view on this important contribution of multinational corporations. In summary, Adam's book is a scholarly Eastern European contribution to the early literature on multinational corporations. As it has not been translated into any of the major languages, such as English or German, it is, however, not very well known outside Hungary.

Adam's second publication, considerably shorter, is based on a different approach.[24] The World Corporation Problematics: Apologetics and Critique is an 80-page survey of the supportive and critical Western literature. The authors are classified on a geographical basis into three major groups: the United States, Western Europe, and Canada. The books, articles, and pamphlets are pre-1970 publications. Consequently, Adam, as before, perceives multinational corporations as chiefly American. He is also far more critical than in his book; he combines selected passages from the Western literature with his own interpretations into harsh ideological statements. The result, at times, is confusing:

> It also reflects, however, the fact that the world corporations--the new supermonopolist elite--feel themselves strong enough to demand a modification of the prevailing power structure ("allocation of resources . . . with no special regard for the country where the parent, by historical accident, is incorporated . . . "), that they would like to get rid of some--or if possible: [sic] of most restrictions imposed upon them by the nation-state, i.e. the collective interests of the class of "national" capitalists; that "global" corporations demand a new charter to pursue their own course of economic aggrandizement, even if it conflicts even more with the interests of other sections of their own class, not to mention other social classes--without wishing, or being able, to dispense with the protection of the nation state.[25]

The survey appears to be a by-product of the research that Adam engaged in for his book. Published in English, the lack of originality and the occasional harsh ideological overtones, however, make it far less useful reading than the book.

In 1971 and 1972, Adam published additional studies dealing with multinational corporations in the leading Hungarian economic journal.[26] The first of these publications, "Runaway Industries and Relocating Corporations in the Capitalistic World Economy," again represents a scholarly effort to explore the economic reasons for worldwide corporate expansion. Well-researched and documented, the study (about 33 journal pages) continues to reflect Adam's perception of multinational corporations as predominantly an American phenomenon. In the follow-up article, published in the same journal at a later date and titled, "New Developments in the Global Optimization of International Corporate Empires," he discusses the expansion of multinational corporations in the developing world as part of their worldwide effort to optimize operations.[27] Similar articles by Adam, dealing with worldwide sourcing and domiciling, appeared in English in Acta Oeconomica, the publication of the Hungarian Academy of Sciences, during 1971 and 1972. In these articles Adam, as before, supports his arguments with Western sources and data. In addition, he also begins to see multinational corporations as more than just the representatives of American capitalism; his analyses also include the international moves of West European, especially West German and Japanese multinationals

Early in the summer of 1974 Adam published a book of readings on multinational corporations. Written in Hungarian and titled World Corporations: A Book of Readings, the publication includes, apart from a general introduction, 14 articles written by a diversified group of authors.[28] The ideological viewpoints are represented by the Soviet economist M. Maksimowa and by the contribution of the economic research section of the British Communist party. These ideological selections are complemented by the critical but analytical writings of Stephen Hymer and Robert Rowthorn. Finally, the entire book is balanced off by Raymond Vernon, Charles Kindleberger, and Rainer Hellman, whose contributions deal with the problems of multinational corporations versus national sovereignty, U.S. direct investment in Europe and Japan, and the European policy toward multinationals. In summary, while the book is critical of multinationals, its overall approach is never unreasonable, and, consequently, those socialist readers who want to find out more about multinational corporations can gain useful insights from the selections presented.

Because of his research and publication efforts, Adam was frequently invited to speak on multinational corporations to various Western audiences. In 1973, the United

Nations invited him to participate in a study of the future
of multinational corporations by the "Group of Eminent
Persons." Consequently, until his unexpected, tragic death
in late June 1974, he was probably the foremost and best
known authority on multinational corporations in socialist
Eastern Europe. His reputation as a scholarly Marxist
analyst and critic was well deserved.

A short but also scholarly discussion of multinational
corporations was published by one of the editors of the
Hungarian economic and management weekly, _Figyelo_, in December 1973.[29] The author, Gyorgy Varga, an economist,
perceives multinational corporations as an American phenomenon. The general tone of the two-part article is critical; the author deplores the worldwide optimizing efforts
of multinationals and points out that because of such efforts competition in world markets is reduced.

In addition to Hungary, studies of multinational corporations were also undertaken in the German Democratic
Republic. The most comprehensive, "International Corpora-
tions--Monopoly Power, Class Struggle," by Katja Nehls,
was published as a research monograph by the Institute for
International Politics and Economics in 1973.[30] The 158-
page publication is based on the classics of Marxism, such
as the collected works of Lenin, and a rather limited collection of Western sources ranging from daily newspapers,
such as the West German _Frankfurter Allgemeine_ to the early
works of Vernon. Apart from a brief section in which the
author deals with the technological aspects of the growth
of multinational corporations, the study is a harsh ideological attack on everything multinational corporations
represent. Nehls perceives the international expansion
of large corporations as chiefly an American phenomenon
and considers such moves a challenge to the working class
the world over. In her introduction she argues:

> With the development of the international corpor-
> ations, the imperialist system created new oppor-
> tunities for social maneuvering and changed the
> conditions under which it can use its economic,
> military and political power to fight socialism
> and to subdue national liberation movements.
>
> The monopolistic control [of the imperialist
> system] over the global capitalistic resources is
> increased [through the multinational corporation]
> which in turn provides the imperialists with a
> better opportunity to execute the scientific-
> technical revolution on their own capitalistic
> terms.

All this, however, means increased danger for
the working class and the non-monopolistic groups
and classes, [because] it makes their defense of
democracy and national sovereignty more difficult.
Consequently, the development of international
corporations also led to the necessity and opportunity to create new and higher forms of interna-
tionalizing the class struggle.[31]

The rest of the study is characterized by similar
statements and arguments. Consequently, while Nehls' study
represents a well-defined socialist point of view, it is
too ideological and rigid to be considered a useful contribution to the literature on multinational corporations.

Another critical, but somewhat less ideological and
rigid East German view was presented by a high official
of the Institute for International Economics and Politics
(the same institute that published the Nehls study) to
the "Group of Eminent Persons" of the United Nations in
Geneva, Switzerland, in November 1973.[32] The paper, titled
"The Impact of Multinational Corporations on International
Economic and Political Relations," consisted of "some
views and proposals" related to the report "Multinational
Corporations in World Development," prepared by the United
Nations. In his introduction the official stated:

The initiative of the United Nations to study the
activities of multinational corporations and their
influence on world developments by a group of Eminent Persons appointed by the Secretary General
meets with the keen interest and the full approval
of my government. It has taken careful note of the
Report "Multinational Corporations in World Development" prepared by the United Nations Secretariat.
This contributes in a comprehensive manner to the
economic, political, and social aspects of the issue, thus promoting further analysis and discussion
and bringing more light into proposals for consequences to be taken.

I am, therefore, glad to avail myself to the
opportunity to present some ideas which we regard
to be significant from the point of view of the
German Democratic Republic on this vital problem
of international relations.[33]

The rest of his paper dealt with the implications of
multinational corporations for the developing world. Like

most socialist observers, the official saw the growth of multinational corporations as a dangerous and chiefly American phenomenon. The final recommendations, representing the official position of the German Democratic Republic, were as follows:

> Despite the immense number of publications concerned with the activities of multinational corporations, there are still a number of economic and political interdependencies waiting for clarification. The Report makes mention of this fact a number of times. This also gives rise to the difficulty of evaluating in a satisfactory manner the efficiency of measures which could be suggested. We believe, therefore, that it would serve the purpose to reinforce studies and information pertaining to such problems. These could possibly include the following:
>
> - The role of multinational corporations in the framework of increasing internationalization of production and international division of labor (existing level and developmental trends).
> - Case studies on the economic and political impacts of the activities of individual multinational corporations respective of a particular multinational corporation in individual developing countries.
> - Hearings and studies on the business strategy and practice of multinational corporations in connection with specific questions such as transfer prices, restrictive business practices, etc.
> - National sovereignty and the role of multinational corporations.
> - The impact of regulations and practices on the part of governments in the home countries of the multinational corporations on the role of these corporations in developing countries.
>
> If the target of these proposals is in accordance with the main goal of our paper, to study problems of the connection between developing countries and multinational corporations, we are nevertheless fully aware of the fact that it is necessary to include questions concerning multinational corporations and the working class and others in further working efforts.[34]

At the same UN meeting, another socialist viewpoint was presented by Romuald Kudlinski, a Polish university professor.[35] Although also critical of multinational corporations, his approach was far more balanced than that of his East German colleague. Kudlinski saw the development of multinational corporations as an American phenomenon and expressed his concern with the influence of these corporations in the developing world. At the same time, he recognized the need for an efficient international division of labor and the potentially useful role of multinational corporations in this process:

> The scientific and technical revolution embraced essentially the same states and nations which were the first to gain the take-off in the 19th century.
>
> The United States played a particular part in promoting science in production processes.
>
> At the same time, from the middle of the 19th and 20th century on, there spread a corporate enterprise that proved particularly useful in mobilizing great capitals and undertaking mass production.
>
> Within the structure of the market economy, great corporations became the only power that enabled the application of the latest scientific and technical achievements in production. They also enjoyed significant financial support of governmental agencies.
>
> Modern techniques and technology cannot be contained within the national boundaries.
>
> Its optimal application requires the use of the international market and international cooperation.
>
> The solutions have been imposed by the logic of market economy. National corporations have been transformed into multinational ones using an exceptionally great expansion capability that stemmed from the technical and capital supremacy. Within the market economy they became the main channel of promoting modern technology.[36]

In his conclusions and recommendations he continued to take a reasonable position:

> 1. In my opinion the most urgent task is to set up a Multinational Corporation Information Centre

under the auspices of the United Nations. This Centre would be expected to collect, analyze and promote information on the activity of the leading multinational corporations particularly in the developing regions. The Information Centre would carry on a case study of agreements and contracts that determine the conditions under which multinational corporations do business in various countries.

2. Following systematic reports from the Information Centre, it would be advisable to arrange periodical meetings of the Group of Eminent Persons during which a current evaluation of multinational corporations influence and activity would be made. It is essential that the work initiated by the publication of the Report entitled Multinational Corporations in World Development should not be discontinued. The reason is that the publishing of the Report and taking of the discussion to the international forum has already played a really promising part.

3. I also consider it an extremely important postulate to be met as quickly as possible, namely, the establishment within the United Nations, of a group of experts providing all countries with a technical aid (in all possible ways) as the countries embark on the accomplishment of development programs with multinational corporations participating.

4. Although the postulate providing for harmonization of national policies toward multinational corporations should be appreciated in glowing terms, it does not stand a chance of quick application the world over as well as in individual economic regions.

5. The suggestion to set up the Centre for Multinational Corporations embracing the corporations that meet the condition of being subjected to international control is extremely interesting.[37]

In addition to academicians, Eastern European mass media and government officials have also expressed new views. A leading Polish newspaper, for example, seemed to prepare the public for close economic ties with multinational corporations:

These corporations often claim they play the role
of stimulators of progress and messengers of
peace.  This is a bit of exaggeration. . . .
These powers without frontiers, as some multinational corporations like to call themselves, are
products of modern capitalism. . . . However,
while not shutting one's eyes to their negative
role, it is impossible to ignore their positive
influence on the world. . . . The cooperation
agreements of socialist states eliminate the negative role of multinational corporations by strict
control clauses.  Under the conditions of planned
economy and with the existence of a strong central
direction (the state), the multinational corporation will have no freedom to cause harm, as happens
in the West.[38]

The monthly organ of the Polish Chamber of Foreign Trade,
Handel Zagraniczny, pointed out that "no country can ignore
the existence of multinational corporations."[39]  Furthermore, the article argued, Polish foreign trade enterprises
do not know enough about the multinational corporation
and that "our foreign trade institutions from top to bot-
tom--from those shaping general strategy to foreign trade
organizations and economic organizations--should also conduct a global policy. . . . We have to prepare ourselves
for coexistence with monopolies."[40]

An even stronger statement concerning economic cooperation and the potential role of multinational corporations in socialist Eastern Europe was made by President
Ceausescu of Romania:

It is true we have also decided to resort, in relations of international economic cooperation, to
the organization of joint companies both in Romania and in other countries.  We have set out to
do this bearing in mind the new development conditions of the world economy and the need for new
forms of economic relations--namely, direct cooperation in production.  This allows for a broader
expansion and more enduring economic relations
with other states and, at the same time, the possibility of introducing advances of contemporary
science and technology into production more
rapidly.[41]

In Czechoslovakia the leading economic weekly, Hospo-darske Noviny, published an article in 1973 in which a government official argued that the country's industrial organizations have not explored the opportunities of set-ting up projects with multinational corporations who have both the technology and markets needed by Czechoslovakia.[42] At a later date, Prime Minister Lubomir Strougal stated that "[Czechoslovakia] should develop economic relations with the capitalist countries more intensively and purpose-fully. We look for possibilities of advantageously expand-ing industrial cooperation . . . and also study other forms of economic cooperation."[43]

Although the Bulgarian government made it very clear that "joint ventures are not permitted under the Bulgarian constitution and that their formation is not to be ex-pected," the government encouraged industry to increase the number of contacts with multinational corporations.[44] To promote such contacts, various organizational changes were introduced throughout the Bulgarian economy.

The topic of doing business with multinational corpor-ations was also discussed during several CMEA meetings. An informal joint position of all CMEA member countries, for example, was developed during a trade symposium held in Moscow in 1972. The consensus of the meeting was that it is important and useful for CMEA countries to deal with multinational corporations and that it might be useful, at some future date, to develop "customs-free zones or en-claves for locating joint manufacturing ventures with West-ern firms."[45] Such isolation of foreign ventures might be an ideologically acceptable way for those countries that do not yet permit equity-based joint ventures (Bulgaria, Czechoslovakia, and the German Democratic Republic) to de-velop closer economic ties with multinationals.

The changing views on multinational corporations in socialist Eastern Europe received substantial support in 1973. First, the Soviet publication Mirovaya Economica i Mezhdunarodniye Otnosheniya (World Economics and Interna-tional Relations), made the following observation:

> It is highly probable that in the years to come
> the development of the world economy will continue
> to be marked by a tendency toward the growth of
> large-batch and mass production, and of the opti-
> mal size of enterprises, the appearance of ever
> new kinds of manufacturers, and increased costs
> of research. These processes will, without
> doubt, make international specialization in pro-

duction and coordination of production and research programs of countries and individual enterprises increasingly beneficial.[46]

Then later in the year, Jerman M. Gvishiani, deputy
chairman of the Soviet Union's Council of Ministers for
Science and Technology, stated in San Francisco at the
closing session of the International Industrial Conference,
attended by 650 industrialists from 75 countries, that

multinational corporations will find an enthusias-
tic host in the Soviet Union [because] the economic relations between the Soviet Union and the
Western economies is passing over from sporadic
commercial deals to a planned and programmed economic cooperation on a stable and long-term basis. One can hardly overestimate both the economic and social implications of this tendency.[47]

Such positive views issued by Soviet leaders undoubtedly
influence the Eastern European economic policy makers.

## SUMMARY

Over the last few years the Eastern European socialist economies emerged as an important group in world trade,
both as producers and consumers, although their share in
total world trade does not correspond to their share in
total world output. With the shift in emphasis from extensive to intensive growth, their need for sophisticated
Western technology, products, and management know-how has
considerably increased. The current East-West trade pattern, however, is highly assymetrical and cannot generate
the hard currency needed to obtain such technology, products, and know-how.
As a result, the Eastern European socialist economies
are restructuring their trade relations with the West and
are increasingly participating in the international division of labor. In general, this means closer economic ties
with the highly industrialized countries of the Western
world, as, for example, the United States, the Federal Republic of Germany, Japan, and others. As the multinational
corporations based in these countries play a key role in
the international transfer of technology and know-how,
such closer ties mean closer contacts with multinational
corporations.

In the past, official views of multinational corporations in the Eastern European socialist economies were
based on hostile ideological considerations alone.  The
socialist governments considered multinational corporations
as chiefly American political and economic tools whose
major aim was to realize the worldwide imperialist aims of
U.S. capitalists.  While most Eastern European governments
and academic observers (despite the gradually changing
evidence) still consider multinational corporations as
mostly American, and while they still perceive them as the
most powerful capitalist forms of business organization,
in most socialist countries the realities of economic life
forced the adoption of less rigid views.  The new views,
in general, are not very different from those expressed by
the United Nations, the International Labor Organization,
the European Economic Community, the U.S. Congress, and
various national governments in both the industrialized
and developing world.  They are critical, but at the same
time, no longer include an out-of-hand dismissal of the
potential contributions multinational corporations can
make to the economic development of the Eastern European
region.  In some countries--for example, Romania, Poland,
and Hungary--such potential contributions are mentioned
by high-level government officials in speeches, articles,
and interviews.  Even the leaders of the German Democratic
Republic are beginning to take a milder position.  In February 1974, for example, Business International held its
first governmental roundtable in East Berlin.  The roundtable was attended by, among others, the Prime Minister
of the GDR, the Minister of Foreign Trade, and 70 top executives representing more than 50 multinational corporations residing in the United States, United Kingdom, Japan,
Sweden, Switzerland, and Italy.

It appears that, encouraged by the positive views of
multinational corporations held by the Soviet Union, the
Eastern European socialist governments are paving the way
for closer economic ties with such corporations.

NOTES

1.  Fortune, no. 3 (September 1973), p. 164.
2.  Computed from Business International, December 7,
1973; and U.S. Department of Commerce, Bureau of East-West
Trade, Selected U.S.S.R. and Eastern European Economic
Data (Washington, D.C.:  U.S. Government Printing Office,
June 1973).

3. This section is based on Thomas A. Wolf, East-West Economic Relations and the Multinational Corporation, Occasional Paper no. 5 (Washington, D.C.: Center for Multinational Studies, July 1973), pp. 14-25.

4. UN Economic Commission for Europe, Analytical Report on Industrial Co-operation Among ECE Countries (E/ECE/844), May 4, 1973.

5. Ibid.

6. Figyelo, October 3, 1973, p. 8. These data are for all CMEA member countries including the Soviet Union.

7. Ibid., p. 8. For CMEA as a whole.

8. Figyelo, September 12, 1973, p. 8. The estimate was made by the UN Economic Commission for Europe (for CMEA as a whole).

9. For a discussion of the various reforms see Radoslav Selucky, Economic Reforms in Eastern Europe: Political Background and Economic Significance (New York: Praeger, 1972).

10. See Geza Peter Lauter, The Manager and Economic Reform in Hungary (New York: Praeger, 1972).

11. Nepszabadsag (People's Freedom), September 22, 1968. This is a Hungarian daily.

12. Figyelo, February 21, 1973, p. 21.

13. For a detailed discussion of CMEA see Sandor Ausch, Theory and Practice of CMEA Cooperation (Budapest: Academic Publishing House, 1972). For an exposition of bilateralism and its problems see Jozef M. P. van Brabant, Bilateralism and Structural Bilateralism in Intra-CMEA Trade (Rotterdam: University Press, 1973).

14. Ausch, op. cit., p. 77.

15. Wolf, op. cit., p. 24.

16. Business International Eastern Europe Report, December 15, 1972), p. 167.

17. Heinrich Machowski, "Toward a Socialist Economic Integration of Eastern Europe," in Sylvia Sinanian, Istvan Deak, and Peter C. Ludz, eds., Eastern Europe in the 1970's (New York: Praeger, 1972), pp. 189-200.

18. Figyelo, October 10, 1973, p. 8.

19. UN Economic Commission for Europe, op. cit.

20. Business International Eastern Europe Report, March 23, 1973, p. 86.

21. Figyelo, August 1, 1973, p. 4.

22. Business Week, December 1, 1973, p. 4.

23. Gyorgy Adam, Amerika Europaban: Vallalatbirodalmak a Vilaggazdasagban (America in Europe: Corporate Empires in the World Economy) (Budapest: Akademiai Konyvkiado [Academic Publishing House], 1970).

24. Gyorgy Adam, <u>The World Corporation Problematics:</u> <u>Apologetics and Critique</u> (Budapest: Hungarian Scientific Council for World Economy, 1971).

25. Ibid., p. 7.

26. Gyorgy Adam, "Szokeveny iparagak es elvandorlo vallalatok a tokes vilaggazdasagban" ("Runaway Industries and Relocating Corporations in the Capitalistic World-Economy"), <u>Kozgazdasagi Szemle</u> (<u>Economic Review</u>), September-October 1971), pp. 1066-81 and 1185-1203.

27. Gyorgy Adam, "A nemzetkozi vallalatbirodalmak globalis optimilizalasanak ujabb fejlemenyei" ("New Developments in the Global Optimization of the International Corporate Empires"), <u>Kozgazdasagi Szemle</u> (<u>Economic Review</u>), July-August 1972, pp. 944-58.

28. Gyorgy Adam, <u>Vilagkonszernek: Valogatas</u> (<u>World Corporations: A Book of Readings</u>) (Budapest: Kozgazdasagies Jogi Konyvkiado [Economic and Legal Publishing House], 1974).

29. Gyorgy Varga, "Transznacionalis vallalatok es a vilaggazdasag" ("Transnational Corporations and the World Economy"), <u>Figyelo</u>, December 12 and 19, 1973, pp. 7 and 8.

30. Habil Katja Nehls, "Internationale Konzerne--Monopolmacht, Klassenkampf," <u>IPW-Forschungshefte</u> (Institute fur Internationale Politik und Wirtschaft, DDR): 8. Jahrgang, Heft 1/1973.

31. Ibid., p. 7.

32. Horst Heininger, "The Impact of Multinational Corporations on International Economic and Political Relations," unpublished paper (Berlin, GDR: Institute for International Politics and Economics, 1973).

33. Ibid., p. 1.

34. Ibid., p. 11.

35. Romuald Kudlinski, "Some Problems of the Multinational Corporations: A Few Sidenotes on the Report Issued by the U.N. Department of Economic and Social Affairs," unpublished paper (Warsaw: Institute for Economic Sciences, University of Warsaw, 1973).

36. Ibid., pp. 5-6.

37. Ibid., pp. 9-10. It should be noted that in its final report the Group recommended actions that were very similar to Professor Kudlinski's. See UN Economic and Social Council, <u>The Impact of Multinational Corporations on the Development Process and on International Relations</u> (E/5500), June 12, 1974.

38. <u>Business International Eastern Europe Report</u>, September 21, 1973, p. 275.

39. <u>Business International Eastern Europe Report</u>, May 18, 1973, p. 140.

40. Ibid., p. 40.

41. John Pearson, "Inside Romania: A Talk with Ceausescu," _Business Week_, December 1, 1973, p. 44.

42. _Business International Eastern Europe Report_, November 2, 1973, p. 319.

43. _Business International Eastern Europe Report_, January 11, 1973, p. 4.

44. _Business International Eastern Europe Report_, June 15, 1973, p. 167.

45. _Business International Eastern Europe Report_, December 1, 1972, p. 158.

46. _Business International Eastern Europe Report_, April 6, 1973, p. 95.

47. The New York _Times_, September 22, 1973, p. 37.

# 3

## THE EMERGING
## RELATIONSHIP

The term most widely used to describe the newly emerging relationship between the Western world and the Eastern European socialist economies is "industrial cooperation." Where and when the term was coined and what precisely it means is difficult to say, although it appears that the term was first used by the socialist economies who were trying to summarily describe the various types of economic ties that have developed during the late 1960s and early 1970s.

The 1973 report of the UN Economic Commission for Europe--based on an extensive study--dealing with industrial cooperation in general, and early East-West industrial cooperation in particular, explained and defined the concept in the following manner:

> For the purposes of the present study it is necessary to have recourse to what may be called a "working definition" of industrial co-operation. The forms of east-west economic relationships under study are of comparatively recent origin--in general, they seldom go back further than 8 to 10 years--and no internationally settled definition has yet emerged. As a result, different meanings are attached to the expression by businessmen, officials and commentators in different countries. Moreover, broader or more restrictive definitions may be used according to the purpose that they are intended to serve; the definition appropriate for statistical records, for example, might be considered quite unsuitable by custom or fiscal administrators. The difficulties in

the way of elaborating a definition suitable for all of these multiple purposes are formidable. No attempt has been made to resolve them here, since definitions for use in international relations are best left to government experts with a specific purpose in mind. Accordingly, the following working definition is merely intended to identify the set of economic relationships considered in this report:

> Industrial co-operation in an east-west context denoted the economic relationships and activities arising from (a) contracts extending over a number of years between partners belonging to different economic systems which go beyond the straightforward sale or purchase of goods and services to include a set of complementary or reciprocally matching operations (in production, in the development and transfer of technology, in marketing, etc.); and from (b) contracts between such partners which have been identified as industrial co-operation contracts by Governments in bilateral or multilateral agreements.[1]

Based on this explanation and definition, the report also spelled out the kinds of economic relationships that industrial cooperation entails:

1. Licensing with full or partial payment by the licensee in products manufactured.
2. Supplying of complete plants or production lines (turn-key projects) with full or partial payment in products manufactured.
3. Co-production based on specialization.
4. Sub-contracting.
5. Contractual joint ventures for production, marketing and R & D.
6. Contractual joint ventures in third countries.

The number of East-West cooperation agreements was estimated by the commission to be around 600 in 1973, with coproduction based on specialization the most widely used form. Licensing with full or partial payment in products manufactured was the second most widely used form, contractual joint ventures in the West third, the supplying of complete plants or production lines in fourth, and subcontracting in fifth place. Contractual joint ventures in third countries came last. Most cooperation agreements were reached in the machine industries; in some Eastern European countries, as, for example, Hungary, 10-15 percent of the machines exported to the West were produced under such agreements.

On the socialist side, Poland and Hungary; on the Western side, the Federal Republic of Germany, France, the United Kingdom, and Italy were the most active participants.

The motives for East-West industrial cooperation were identified by the commission as follows:

1. New trading opportunities.
2. Differential factor costs.
3. Transfer of technology.
4. Stability in the development of economic relations.
5. Specialization and economies of scale.
6. External economies.
7. Balanced financing and foreign exchange economies.
8. Administrative customs and related facilities.
9. Transport costs.
10. Miscellaneous advantages related to particular technologies, markets, enterprises, or products.

In listing the motives for industrial cooperation the commission also pointed out:

It would be misleading if the foregoing catalogue of motives for industrial co-operation conveyed the impression that they are all of equal importance and accessibility to enterprises engaging in co-operation. Depending on circumstances--such as the technological or product characteristics just referred to--some may not occur at all. In its inquiries, the secretariat tried to ascertain how enterprises themselves rated the strength of various advantages as a motive for engaging in industrial cooperation. In most cases, western partners attached high value to savings in labour costs and also to the reliability and quality of their partners' production. In a number of cases, however, the technology of the eastern partner was rated as an equally potent motive. For most eastern partners, the highest value was attached to the opening of new marketing opportunities and the possibility of obtaining technological benefits.[2]

A marked characteristic of early East-West industrial
cooperation--not specifically mentioned in the UN report--
was the absence of equity-based joint ventures in the socialist economies and the low participation rate of multinational corporations and American companies. The major
reasons for this are known; the ideological problems of
accepting Western equity ownership in the socialist economies, the uncertain political relationships between the
Soviet Union and the Eastern Europeans on the one hand and
the Western world on the other, and the tight control exercised by the U.S. government over trade with the socialist world. The UN report shows the effects of such limitations on the nature and relative importance of early
East-West industrial cooperation. Although at the time of
the study approximately 600 agreements were in force, most
were small scale and short term in nature.

By 1973-74, several reasons for the initially limited
nature of East-West industrial cooperation were eliminated
or, at least, recognized as undesirable by the governments
involved. The détente between the Soviet Union and the
United States, the resulting easing of political tensions
(Vietnam), the more flexible economic postures of the Eastern European socialist economies, and the gradual revision
of U.S. trade policies toward the socialist world created
a more conducive atmosphere for the extension of East-West
industrial cooperation. This is not to suggest that no
more problems should be expected; in addition to the remaining political uncertainties, the unresolved nature,
for example, of many of the technical details of closer
economic ties are harbingers of future misunderstandings.
It seems reasonable to argue, however, that problems of a
technical nature are more apt to be solved through trial-
error procedures and experience than the fundamental political issues involved in the détente.

## THE ROLE OF MULTINATIONAL
## CORPORATIONS

The 1973 study of the United Nations on "Multinational
Corporations in World Development" concluded that "the
need to exercise control is reflected in the preference of
multinational corporations for wholly owned subsidiaries,
although control can at times be achieved through joint
ventures and even min.rity positions."[3] The author of
another study argued in a similar vein:

Developing economies pose a special set of dilemmas for international [multinational] firms. In many instances, these firms feel that it is only through the intensive and sustained relationship associated with significant ownership and control that technology can be transplanted effectively and that they can earn an adequate return. Implicit here are certain assumptions, real or imagined, that equity ownership means control of factors affecting long-term profit maximization, such as inter-affiliate pricing, production and marketing logistics, and the maintenance of product standards. They feel under normal licensing arrangements, it is much more difficult to earn what is considered an adequate return from royalties and technical assistance fees, especially if the firm is to maintain its product standards and protect its trade name.[4]

By substituting the term "socialist economies" for "developing economies" these arguments can be equally well applied to the emerging relationship between multinational corporations and the Eastern European socialist economies.

The legal framework for early East-West industrial cooperation did not provide for anything resembling the sort of arrangement multinational corporations prefer. Consequently, the passing of equity joint venture laws first in Romania, then in Hungary was an important development. (See Appendix for the Hungarian Law as an illustration.) In permitting 49 percent equity ownership by foreigners, these two pioneering socialist countries have offered what multinational corporations want in large-scale long-term projects: ownership (that is, control) and a continuous sharing of profits. While all the details of equity joint venture relationships have not yet been worked out, the passing of the laws indicates that Romania and Hungary are seriously interested in stable, long-term economic relationships. Although Bulgaria, Czechoslovakia, the German Democratic Republic, and Poland have not yet passed similar laws, in time--except perhaps for the GDR-- they are likely to do so. Thereby multinational corporations will eventually be provided with a uniform set of operating conditions throughout the Eastern European region.

# BENEFITS TO MULTINATIONAL
CORPORATIONS

As discussed in Chapter 1, the general long-range aim of multinational corporations is sales maximization based on comparative advantages in technology and/or management and on risk aversion considerations. The following potential benefits of closer economic ties with the Eastern European socialist economies are important contributions to the accomplishment of this aim.

## Stable Domestic Political-
## Economic Conditions

The realization of the long-range aim, as defined previously, is based on continuous planning in all areas of corporate activity. Good planning that is the development of realistic and efficient objectives, policies, and programs, however, is possible only in relatively stable political and economic environments. Domestic political and economic uncertainty has been widespread in both the industrialized and developing world over the last decade. The economic problems in the United Kingdom during 1973-74, the Mid-East war of 1973, the political and economic upheavals in Chile the same year, the urban guerrilla activities in Argentina, and numerous similar events are a good illustration of the type of difficulties that can make good planning and, consequently, the optimization of worldwide operations an enormously complex, if not impossible, task.

It could be argued that such political and economic uncertainties are the characteristics of free societies; consequently, they have to be accepted as the price of freedom. While for a number of uncertainties, such as economic slowdowns and strikes, the argument holds true, the majority of worldwide problems faced by multinational corporations during the last few years were of the violent kind that had little to do with the basic issues of freedom. Such problems occurred because some governments were--and still are--unable to guarantee even a modicum of political, economic, and social stability. The events in Argentina during 1973-74 are a case in point; the tragic execution of Ford Company executive John A. Swint by guerrillas, the ransom payment of $14.2 million by Exxon for the life of refinery manager Victor E. Samuelson, the extortion of $1 million from the Ford Company, the death warning issued

to all Ford Company executives, and the wholesale kidnaping
of other major corporation executives have created an atmosphere in which routine business operations are impossible. Even in relatively stable and prosperous Mexico, multinationals, especially American, are no longer entirely
safe. In February 1974, seven bombs exploded in Pepsi-Cola
and Union Carbide plants in Guadalajara, and in a Coca-Cola
plant in Oaxaca. Although no human life was lost, damage
was considerable.

The Eastern European socialist governments closely
control both political and economic activities. The economic reforms of the late 1960s did not affect the undis-
puted leading role of the Communist parties and, although
the reforms changed the nature and scope of enterprise activities, the overall structure and growth of the socialist
economies is still centrally planned and guided. Thus, as
long as the socialist governments guarantee the survival
of multinational corporations and are willing to offer
attractive economic incentives, the political and economic
stability prevailing in the Eastern European socialist
countries provide multinational corporations with more desirable operational environments than those offered by some
Western European and most developing countries.


Stability and Quality of Labor

Stable labor conditions in the Eastern European socialist economies are, of course, a result of the prevailing political and economic conditions. The general absence of labor strife in these countries, however, is so
important to multinational corporations that it merits
separate discussion.

As a result of astute political leadership, improved
organization, and aggressive policies the labor unions of
most industrialized countries have, over the years, developed into powerful and influential pressure groups. The
1974 economic crisis in the United Kingdom, for example,
was caused by a clash between the conservative government
and the mining union. The West German labor unions, un-
demanding and cooperative for a quarter of a century, became aggressive and demanding during the early 1970s. Inflationary pressures and the resulting wage settlements
led to wildcat strikes in 24 industrial firms in early
1973. Close to 40,000 workers of such major companies as
Volkswagon, Hoesch, and Klockner were involved. Even the
docile and mostly unorganized "guestworkers" from Turkey

and other developing countries began to assert their rights. During the summer of 1973 about 12,000 Turkish workers of the German Ford Company revolted against working conditions and succeeded in stopping production throughout the entire plant for several days. Led by an energetic and articulate Turkish compatriot and supported by several dozen Maoist West German university students, this wildcat strike opened up an entirely new chapter in the history of the postwar West German labor movement. It should also be noted that while order was eventually restored, for a time management, the state, and the federal government lost control over events.

By 1973, the International Federation of Chemical, Food and Metalworking Unions was actively organizing united actions against European multinational corporations. Their objective is to support the workers of multinational companies in one country by putting pressure on the affiliates in other countries. The Michelin Company, one of the biggest French multinationals, for example, agreed in 1973 to discuss with unions its plans for modernizing five Italian plants. Michelin, which employs 15,000 workers making tires in Italy, agreed to such action after its plants in France and England were struck by workers. The nine councils of the World Auto Council of the International Metalworkers Federation represent unions in the worldwide plants of General Motors, Ford, Chrysler, Volkswagon and Daimler-Benz, British Leyland, Renault-Peugeot, Fiat, Citroen, Toyota, and Nissan. Finally, in 1973 the European Economic Community's Executive Commission adopted proposals to improve job benefits and, most of all, to protect European workers against multinational corporations in the community's labor market. More specifically, the proposal called for minimum standards of protection for all workers against mass dismissals if and when multinational companies close factories where labor costs are on the rise and move production to parts of the community where cheaper labor is available. The proposal is weighted in labor's favor; as Patrick Hillary, the community's Commissioner for Labor Policy, stated: "Europe must respond positively to the anxieties of its workers so we certainly paid more heed to suggestions from trade unions than from representatives of management."[5]

Finally, it should be pointed out that in the future such pressures are likely to intensify. The drive by labor unions in Western Europe to make employee pensions uniform and compulsory throughout the area have already resulted in Hewlett-Packard and the Gillette Company increasing their pension fund coverage to eight and nine countries respectively. The drive for labor coownership of industrial enterprises (reaching a maximum of 50 percent), in Denmark, Sweden, and the Netherlands and the struggle over what form codetermination should take in the Federal Republic of Germany are indications of a strong and unabating trend. In the spring of 1974, Prime Minister Olaf Palme of Sweden proposed a law that would require multinational corporations to submit all foreign expansion plans to the government, which would base its decision on whether or not the expansion would impair Swedish employment. While socially desirable, such trends can easily worsen the already tenuous relationship between multinational corporations and the various national and international labor organizations.

The Eastern European socialist labor unions, although more independent and active than during the prereform years, do not consider multinational corporations as adversaries with whom they have to battle for better pay and working conditions every inch of the way. All details of labor-management relations in general, and of working conditions in particular, are worked out and agreed upon by the socialist governments and multinational corporations beforehand. The responsibility of labor unions, if at all, does not extend beyond the administration of the contractual agreements. Consequently, labor strikes or slowdowns and other upheavals in the Eastern European countries against multinational corporations are almost inconceivable.

Finally, it is also important to point out that the quality of labor both in terms of skills and work-discipline is quite high in the Eastern European socialist countries. It is true that absenteeism and low level of work motivation are currently widespread in some countries, as, for example, Hungary and Poland, but this is the result of the existing working conditions and ineffective incentive systems and not of the inherent characteristics of Hungarian or Polish workers. Advanced technology, better working conditions, and improved incentive systems provided by multinational corporations could, in a very short time, bring out the best qualities of a very able and productive labor force. There is ample evidence to support such contention; the prewar labor force of Czechoslovakia, for example, was one of the most productive in Europe. Properly motivated, it built up one of the most developed European economies of that era. In addition, the problem of illiteracy as known in many developing countries is nonexistent in the Eastern European socialist countries; the compulsory basic education systems are comprehensive and of good qual-

ity.  The reformed apprenticeship systems and technical
schools provide trade specialization opportunities to the
graduates of the basic educational system who do not wish
to go on to higher education.  The result is an intelligent
and able labor pool that just needs to be tapped in an effective and humane way to become reliable and productive.


## Lower Production Costs

Although detailed comparative production cost data de-
scribing conditions in the Eastern European socialist economies and the rest of the world are not available, there
seems to be general agreement among students of East-West
economic relations that production costs in the Eastern
Europe socialist economies are generally lower than in the
developed Western world.  Especially the inflationary wage
rises, outstripping productivity increases, of the last
few years are important in this respect.  During 1967-73,
average pay increases in Sweden amounted to 100 percent.[6]
During 1973-74, most of the Western European economies en-
dured annual inflation ranging from about 7 to 15 percent.
As could be expected, union wage demands were designed to
prevent or at least to minimize the ensuing painful loss
in real income.  In February 1974, for example, striking
public service employees in the Federal Republic of Germany
demanded and received a 13 percent pay increase.  As a consequence, other big German unions, most notably the 4 million member metalworkers, were also pushing for a similar
increase in wages.  Such developments prompted D. W. von
Menges, Chairman of the Board of the European Economic Community's largest machine producer (Gutehoffnungshutte) to
argue that "in the long run we can continue to produce in
the Federal Republic [of Germany] only technologically
highly sophisticated products.  Simple mass-production
will be uneconomical, because wages are too high.  All
such production will have to be moved to foreign [that is,
low wage] countries."[7]
In its July 1974 "Annual Economic Outlook," the Organization for Economic Cooperation and Development pointed
out that such trends are going to continue in the future,
because "inflation will be kept going by a wage-price
spiral, as different groups in the community struggle to
offset the large changes in relative prices that have occurred and to maintain their real incomes."
Although as the Eastern European socialist economies
are getting more involved with the world economy, they are

going to find it increasingly more difficult to isolate
themselves from worldwide inflation. Until now the socialist governments have succeeded in keeping domestic inflation down to a much lower level than the 7 to 15 percent
level in the West. Accordingly, wages in the Eastern European socialist economies are under much less pressure. It
could be argued, of course, that labor costs in most developing countries are even lower than in the Eastern European
socialist economies and that because of this multinational
corporations could better minimize production costs if they
set up plants in such economies. Ignoring all other possible considerations, such as proximity to markets, this argument, however, does not hold true, because the quality
of labor in most developing countries cannot be compared
to that of, for example, Czechoslovakia, Hungary, or Poland.
Consequently, it seems reasonable to propose that wage dif-
ferentials between developing countries and the Eastern
European socialist economies are more than offset by the
better quality and, therefore, high productivity of Eastern
European labor.

In taking advantage of lower production costs in the
Eastern European socialist economies, multinational corporations, thus, could obtain benefits. A West German company,
for example, reported that its cooperation agreement with
a Hungarian industrial enterprise resulted in 15 to 20
percent lower production costs than those it would have had
to incur if it had limited its production to the Federal
Republic of Germany, or other Western European countries.[8]

On the other hand, it needs to be pointed out that,
as long as the Eastern European socialist governments,
through various administrative means, continue to shield
their economies from worldwide inflation and continue to
maintain artificial price relationships, some of the production cost advantages in these countries might be the
result of such artificial prices and, consequently, cost
distortions.[9] Furthermore, the recently developed policy
of some socialist governments as, for example, that of the
Romanian to require foreign joint venture partners to pay
relatively high so-called "export wages" in hard currency
into a special fund, introduces additional complications.
(These wages are high even relative to Western Europe;
workers, of course, get only a part of the wages in local
currency.)

New Markets

During the last decade, multinational corporations moved into most of the available markets in Western Europe, Latin America, the Far East, and, to a more limited degree, in the Middle East and Africa. Consequently, the Eastern European socialist economies are among the last few major market areas of the world where multinational corporations have not yet established themselves.

The market potential in these countries for most industrial goods and, to some extent, even for certain types of consumer products, is considerable. As pointed out before, the switch from an extensive to an intensive economic growth strategy requires sophisticated industrial equipment and technology developed and marketed mostly by multinational corporations. Other developments, such as higher standards of living and increased travel to the West, have resulted in new, more sophisticated consumption patterns in most socialist countries. Eastern European customers, especially in Hungary and Czechoslovakia, can no longer be satisfied by domestic manufacturers whose product assortments, in most cases, lack both the quality and choice desired.

Table 3.1 presents a set of data that can be used as market indicators for the Eastern European socialist economies. While these data are not all-encompassing, they provide a reasonable amount of insight into market structures.

As pointed out in the previous chapter, in 1972 about 60 percent of the total $36 billion world trade share of the Eastern European socialist economies represented intra-CMEA trade. Consequently, multinational corporations that enter individual Eastern European markets can enter additional markets in the region through bilateral intra-CMEA trade agreements without encountering additional restrictions.

Finally, new markets can be opened up and additional trade restrictions can be avoided by multinational corporations through bilateral trade and cooperation agreements that the Eastern European socialist economies maintain with developing countries. The best candidates for inclusion in such trade agreements are products, such as machines and industrial equipment, needed by the developing countries for industrialization. Hungary, for example, increased its exports to developing countries by 79 percent during the 1968-72 period; during the same time the share of machines and industrial equipment in the total increased

TABLE 3.1

Market Indicators for the Eastern European Socialist Economies, 1972

| | Bul-garia | Czecho-slo-vakia | German Democratic Republic | Hun-gary | Poland | Ro-mania |
|---|---|---|---|---|---|---|
| **Population** | | | | | | |
| Total, 1971 (million) | 8.6 | 14.5 | 17.0 | 10.4 | 33.1 | 20.8 |
| Past five years--percent increase | 3.2 | 1.2 | -0.2 | 1.9 | 3.5 | 7.7 |
| UN forecast, 1980 | 9.2 | 15.8 | 17.7 | 10.8 | 36.6 | 22.4 |
| **GNP** | | | | | | |
| Total, 1972 (billion $) | 13.5[a] | 35.2[a] | 43.3[a] | 17.2[a] | 52.0[a] | 28.8[a] |
| Percent five-year increase (constant prices) | 42.1 | 19.3 | 23.7 | 18.4 | 26.8 | 37.8 |
| National Income | | | | | | |
| Total, 1972 (billion $) | 6.1[b] | 21.1[b] | 37.5[b] | 11.5[b] | 42.9[b] | 11.8[f] |
| Percent five-year increase (current) | 44.5 | 46.7 | 29.1 | 53.7 | 56.4 | n.a. |
| Per capita, 1972 ($) | 741 | 1,455 | 2,208 | 1,110 | 1,296 | 570[f] |
| **Manufacturing as Percent of Domestic Product** | | | | | | |
| 1971 | 50.8 | 61.0[c,d] | 63.7 | 41.2 | 50.6 | 61.1[g] |
| 1966 | 44.8 | 63.4[c,d] | 61.8 | 57.6 | 51.1 | n.a. |
| **Average Hourly Earnings in Manufacturing** | | | | | | |
| 1971 ($) | 0.36 | 0.74 | 1.08 | 0.44 | 0.64 | 0.42[h] |
| Percent five-year increase (current) | 29.6 | 36.0 | 19.0 | 28.5 | 22.1 | 22.0[i] |
| **Imports** | | | | | | |
| From United States | | | | | | |
| 1972 f.o.b. (million $) | 3 | 49 | 15 | 23 | 112 | 69 |
| Percent five-year increase | -20 | 158 | -43 | 188 | 84 | 313 |
| From EEC | | | | | | |
| 1972 f.o.b. (million $) | 236 | 703 | 337 | 593 | 1,075 | 684 |
| Percent five-year increase | 44 | 66 | 111 | 119 | 97 | 47 |
| From Japan | | | | | | |
| 1972 f.o.b. (million $) | 21 | 15 | 48 | 11 | 89 | 48 |
| Percent five-year increase | -14 | 150 | 1,427 | 175 | 1,410 | 78 |
| Total | | | | | | |
| 1972 c.i.f. (million $) | 2,548[e] | 4,662[e] | 5,905[e] | 3,154 | 5,335[e] | 2,910[j] |
| Percent five-year increase | 62 | 74 | 80 | 78 | 102 | 88[j] |
| **Total Exports** | | | | | | |
| 1972 f.o.b. (billion $) | 2,603 | 5,124 | 6,184 | 3,292 | 4,932 | 2,892[j] |
| Percent five-year increase | 79 | 79 | 79 | 93 | 95 | 84[j] |

[a] In constant 1970 dollars.
[b] Net material product
[c] Including mining and quarrying
[d] Including electricity, gas, and water.
[e] f.o.b.
[f] Estimated, see Table 2.1 footnote.
[g] Anuarul Statistic al Republicii Socialiste Romania, 1973.
[h] Estimated from average monthly salary of lei 1461; see Anuarul Statistic al Republicii Socialiste Romania, 1973.
[i] Estimated from data contained in Anuarul Statistic al Republicii Social-iste Romania, 1973.
[j] Anuarul Statistic al Republicii Socialiste Romania, 1973, p. 467. Five-year increase estimated on the basis of the 1965-72 period.

Sources: Business International, December 7, 1973, pp. 389-90; and Anua-rul Statistic al Republicii Socialiste Romania, 1973, p. 467.

three times as fast as the share of other products.[10]  Recently the Hungarians have also been engaged in several turnkey projects.  In India, for example, they built a pharmaceutical manufacturing plant that produces, among other things, the entire vitamin B-12 requirement of India. In Iran, Hungarian experts assembled a poultry processing plant, while an entire clothing factory was put up in Egypt.  Hungary is currently also building two (total value about $4,250,000) canneries in Algeria.  There are plans to establish an aluminum rolling mill and other factories in Ceylon.  On the other hand, due to technological and financial limitations, many Hungarian enterprises are not able to participate in such projects.  This prompted a Hungarian economist to state that such problems could be solved "through joint efforts with large capitalistic firms with whom both the risks and profits of such projects could be shared."[11]

Table 3.2 presents a list of countries with whom the various Eastern European socialist economies maintained bilateral clearing (trade) agreements at the end of 1972.

Information concerning the magnitude of Eastern European economic credits and grants to developing countries between 1968 and 1972 is presented in Table 3.3.  This and the previous table are indicative of the number, size, and location of possible new markets that could be opened up by multinational corporations after an initial entry into the Eastern European socialist economies.  As can be seen from these data, Eastern European economic credits and grants, far more trade oriented than those of the Soviet Union, were concentrated (about 60 percent of total) in Middle Eastern and South Asian countries--areas in which, except for oil exploration, multinational corporations are currently not doing too much business.


New Technology


In the past, sophisticated new technology had been developed almost exclusively in the highly industrialized countries of the West, and then transferred through trade and other means to the rest of the world.  While the rest of the world in general and the Eastern European socialist economies in particular are still chiefly on the receiving end of the international transfer of technology, recent evidence indicates that the Eastern European countries are beginning to develop new applications for existing technology and new technology itself.  Table 3.4 presents data supporting this conclusion.

TABLE 3.2

Bilateral Clearing (Trade) Agreements Between Developing
Countries and the Eastern European Socialist Economies
at the End of 1972

| | Bul-garia | Czecho-slo-vakia | German Democratic Republic | Hun-gary | Po-land | Ro-mania |
|---|---|---|---|---|---|---|
| Afghanistan | x | x | | | x | |
| Algeria | x | x | | x | x | x |
| Bangladesh | x | x | | x | x | x |
| Bolivia | x | | | x | x | |
| Brazil | x | | x | x | x | x |
| Cambodia | x | x | x | | x | |
| Chad | | | | | | |
| Chile | x | | | | x | |
| Colombia | x | | x | x | x | x |
| Cyprus | x | x | x | x | x | x |
| Ecuador | x | | x | x | x | x |
| Egypt | x | x | x | x | x | x |
| Ghana | x | | | | x | x |
| Greece | x | x | x | x | x | x |
| Guinea | x | x | x | x | x | x |
| India | x | x | x | x | x | x |
| Iran | x | x | | x | x | x |
| Iraq | | | | | | |
| Israel | x | | | x | | |
| Lebanon | | x | x | | x | x |
| Mali | | x | x | x | x | x |
| Mexico | | | | x | x | |
| Morocco | x | x | x | x | x | |
| Nepal | x | | | | x | |
| Pakistan | x | x | | x | x | x |
| Sri Lanka | x | x | x | x | x | x |
| Sudan | | x | x | x | x | |
| Syria | x | | x | x | x | x |
| Turkey | x | x | x | x | x | x |

Source: International Monetary Fund, 24th Annual
Report on Exchange Restrictions, 1973.

69

TABLE 3.3

Eastern European Economic Credits and Grants Extended to
Developing Countries, 1968-72
(million of U.S. $)

| Area and Country | 1968 | 1969 | 1970 | 1971 | 1972 |
|---|---|---|---|---|---|
| Africa | 56 | 11 | 84 | 99 | 209 |
| Algeria | -- | -- | 74 | -- | 150 |
| Ethiopia | -- | -- | -- | -- | -- |
| Ghana | -- | -- | -- | -- | -- |
| Guinea | -- | -- | -- | -- | -- |
| Mali | -- | -- | -- | -- | -- |
| Morocco | 5 | -- | -- | -- | -- |
| Nigeria | -- | -- | -- | 24 | -- |
| Somalia | -- | -- | -- | -- | 2 |
| Sudan | -- | 11 | 10 | 75 | -- |
| Tanzania | -- | -- | -- | -- | 7 |
| Tunisia | 51 | -- | -- | -- | -- |
| Zambia | -- | -- | -- | -- | 50 |
| East Asia | 0 | 12 | 0 | 0 | 0 |
| Burma | -- | -- | -- | -- | -- |
| Cambodia | -- | 12 | -- | -- | -- |
| Indonesia | -- | -- | -- | -- | -- |
| Latin America | 10 | 11 | 51 | 174 | 98 |
| Argentina | 5 | -- | -- | -- | -- |
| Bolivia | -- | -- | 1 | 25 | -- |
| Brazil | -- | -- | -- | -- | -- |
| Chile | 5 | -- | -- | 95 | 20 |
| Colombia | -- | -- | -- | 5 | -- |
| Ecuador | -- | 5 | -- | 5 | -- |
| Peru | -- | 6 | 25 | 44 | 78 |
| Uruguay | -- | -- | 15 | -- | -- |
| Venezuela | -- | -- | 10 | -- | -- |
| Near East/South Asia | 100 | 396 | 53 | 195 | 338 |
| Afghanistan | -- | -- | -- | -- | -- |
| Bangladesh | -- | -- | -- | -- | 25 |
| Egypt | -- | -- | -- | 142 | -- |
| India | -- | 32 | -- | -- | -- |
| Iran | 75 | 200 | -- | -- | 10 |
| Iraq | -- | 125 | 43 | 37 | 200 |
| Pakistan | -- | 8 | 10 | -- | -- |
| Sri Lanka | -- | -- | -- | -- | 10 |
| Syria | 25 | 25 | -- | -- | 93 |
| Turkey | -- | 6 | -- | -- | -- |
| Yemen (Aden) | -- | -- | -- | 16 | -- |
| Yemen (Sana) | -- | -- | -- | -- | -- |

Source: U.S. Department of State, Bureau of Public Affairs,
News Release, August 1973.

TABLE 3.4

Patent Rights Granted to and Received from West European Countries by East European Countries, 1964-71

| | 1964 | 1965 | 1966 | 1967 | 1968 | 1969 | 1970 | 1971 | 1964-67 | 1968-71 | 1964-71 |
|---|---|---|---|---|---|---|---|---|---|---|---|
| **Bulgaria** | | | | | | | | | | | |
| Patents granted | 29 | 28 | 139 | 127 | 137 | 99 | 241 | 186 | 323 | 662 | 985 |
| Patents received | -- | -- | -- | 65 | 76 | 90 | 86 | 112 | 60 | 364 | 424 |
| **Czechoslovakia** | | | | | | | | | | | |
| Patents granted | 255 | 195 | 337 | 453 | 569 | 492 | 696 | 773 | 1,240 | 2,530 | 3,770 |
| Patents received | 804 | 1,163 | 1,319 | 1,332 | 1,185 | 1,250 | 1,100 | 1,136 | 4,618 | 4,671 | 9,289 |
| **German Democratic Re-public** | | | | | | | | | | | |
| Patents granted | -- | 1,238 | 1,520 | 1,266 | -- | 1,151 | 1,792 | 2,442 | 4,024 | 5,385 | 9,409 |
| Patents received | 216 | 496 | 621 | 755 | 1,058 | 578 | 814 | 1,274 | 2,088 | 3,724 | 5,812 |
| **Hungary** | | | | | | | | | | | |
| Patents granted | 206 | 210 | 297 | 347 | 480 | 506 | 514 | 668 | 1,060 | 2,168 | 3,228 |
| Patents received | 301 | 351 | 420 | 454 | 411 | 440 | 492 | 612 | 1,526 | 1,955 | 3,481 |
| **Poland** | | | | | | | | | | | |
| Patents granted | 186 | 247 | 291 | 279 | 298 | 399 | 287 | 414 | 1,003 | 1,398 | 2,401 |
| Patents received | 74 | 157 | 157 | 283 | 148 | 262 | 273 | 258 | 671 | 991 | 1,662 |
| **Romania** | | | | | | | | | | | |
| Patents granted | -- | 213 | 424 | 841 | 200 | 12 | 53 | 164 | 1,478 | 429 | 1,907 |
| Patents received | 94 | 138 | 115 | 169 | 136 | 81 | 160 | 219 | 516 | 596 | 1,112 |

Source: UN Economic Commission for Europe, Analytical Report on Industrial Co-Operation Among ECE Countries (E/ECE/844), May 4, 1973, p. 33.

As can be seen from these data, most of the Eastern European socialist economies, but especially the German Democratic Republic and Czechoslovakia, have over the years granted a substantial number of patents to Western countries. Important technological contributions were also made by Hungary; Electronics Weekly, a British industrial publication, for example, reported from the 1973 Budapest International Fair:

> The Hungarians, like many others, believe the future lies in specializing rather than the comprehensive jamboree--seen in its most ostentatious form in Leipzig. . . . What were described as mark ERC 43 rural terminal [telephone] exchanges with 20 to 80 extensions were, officials said, a product of "socialist integration." The ERC 43 is a member of the family of exchanges operated with common electronic control and capable of setting up rural networks. It is the outcome of Council of Mutual Economic Assistance (CMEA) joint development.
>
> That telephone switching equipment . . . is sent worldwide with export turnover having increased 1000 percent in 10 years.
>
> A considerable proportion of the success is due to the cooperation agreement with the Swedish firm, L. M. Ericsson. In association with the various bodies under the group name Budavox it manufactures urban and rural exchanges, automatic long-distance dialing exchanges and line concentrators.[12]

Another Hungarian company, Temaforg, developed a process for recycling thermoplastic waste material and turning it into heat and acoustic insulating plates. The process is so successful that already 10 Western countries have bought the patent; quite a few more are negotiating for it.

The nature and scope of research and development activities in Hungary is a good illustration of how this important function is performed throughout socialist Eastern Europe. In the spring of 1974, for example, approximately 29,000 Hungarian research and development personnel pursued 15,000 different projects funded by 2.5 percent of national income.[13] While such a large number of projects probably included a certain amount of duplication and some not too well conceived ideas, the previously mentioned examples of technological inventions indicate that on the whole, the end results seem to justify such a vast scope.

Multinational corporations establishing close economic ties with Eastern European socialist economies can thus expect to benefit from the research and development efforts in these countries. Especially research exploring new and more efficient applications for existing technology can be important in this respect, because it can renew the life cycle of numerous existing products manufactured by multinational corporations. The financial and structural limitations on the immediate application of highly sophisticated technology in the Eastern European countries are strong inducements for socialist innovators to search for new and better applications of existing technology for which, among others, the developing countries may also turn out to be important markets. As pointed out before, entry into these markets through the numerous bilateral clearing (trade) arrangements between the socialist countries and the developing world could open up a host of new opportunities for multinational corporations. Such a possibility, however, should not be interpreted as a willingness of Eastern European socialist governments to indiscriminately buy and use dated technology. Any multinational corporation that attempted to sell such technology would quickly find itself permanently locked out of the Eastern European economies.

## BENEFITS TO THE EASTERN EUROPEAN
## SOCIALIST ECONOMIES

Close economic ties between multinational corporations and the socialist economies are a part of the new intensive economic growth strategy of the Eastern European region. More specifically, multinationals can provide the socialist economies with the following benefits.

### Relative Political Independence

It is interesting that the characteristic of multinational corporations that raised so many debates in the Western and developing world, their relative independence of national governments, may turn out to be one of the more desirable features of these large organizations as seen by the Eastern European socialist countries. This does not mean that in the context of various foreign policy and economic development statements the political leaders and economists of these countries are not critical of this particular feature of multinational corporations. Ideo-

logically the relative independence and, consequently, considerable political and economic power of these large corporations cannot be condoned, because "they represent monop-
olistic interests who are in conflict with the world-wide
liberation movement of subjugated people." The discussion
of Eastern European views on multinational corporations in
Chapter 2 presented such ideological arguments. On the
other hand, the Eastern European socialist governments are
pragmatic enough to consider relative political independence
a desirable feature, because it enables them to develop
closer economic ties with capitalist corporations without,
at the same time, having to accept the political influence
of particular capitalist governments. In an era of pronounced political divisions, relatively independent multinational corporations interested chiefly in economic gain,
are more free of ideological fetters than any other kind
of business organization. Of course, multinational corporations must recognize that while the Eastern European
socialist governments are pragmatic enough to use political
independence to their benefit, they are also strong and
ideologically committed enough to immediately crush any
exercise of corporate independence that could negatively
affect their national interests. Although the international
climate during the late 1940s was different from today, and
although all multinational corporations do not act like
ITT did in Hungary 25 years ago, the Hungarian experience
of ITT should be a strong warning to multinational corporations not to exert undue influence when doing business in
the Eastern European socialist economies.[14]


Size

The immense size of multinational corporations can
provide the Eastern European socialist economies with numerous benefits. Foremost among them is the stability of
relationships that large trading partners with contacts
all over the globe can provide. Because of their vast resources, multinational corporations are far less subject
to short-term economic dislocations and can, therefore,
guarantee the kind of stability the Eastern European socialist economies must have in order to effectively pursue
their new, intensive economic growth strategies and to
continually improve their world trade position. Table 3.5
illustrates the relative size of selected multinational
corporations and of the Eastern European socialist economies in terms of 1972 sales and GNP data.

TABLE 3.5

Size of Selected Multinational Corporations Relative
to the Eastern European Socialist Economies, 1972
(billions of U.S. dollars)

| Multinationals | Sales | Socialist Economies | GNP |
|---|---|---|---|
| General Motors[a] | 30.4 | Bulgaria | 13.5 |
| Ford[a] | 20.1 | Czechoslovakia | 35.2 |
| Royal Dutch Shell[b] | 14.0 | German Democratic | |
| General Electric[a] | 10.2 | Republic | 43.3 |
| IBM[a] | 9.5 | Hungary | 17.2 |
| Unilever[a] | 8.8 | Poland | 52.0 |
| | | Romania | 28.8 |

[a]United States.
[b]Netherlands and United Kingdom.

Sources: Fortune, May and September 1973, pp. 220-47
and 202-03; and Business International, December 7, 1973,
p. 390.

As the comparison shows, economic relations between corporations of such enormous size and national economies of
almost similar magnitudes could be called a relationship
between "near equals." Of course, a "near equality" exists
only in terms of the economic measurements chosen for the
purpose of comparison. The political and social significance of nation states as opposed to that of multinational
corporations is not a debatable issue.

While the short-term benefits of close economic ties
with large multinational corporations are substantial, in
the long run, the large size and worldwide involvement of
multinationals is going to create difficulties for the socialist economies. As these economies get more and more
involved in international trade they are going to find that
the most aggressive competitors in global markets are the
same multinational corporations that--in the short run--are
preferred economic partners. (Of course, the same holds
true for the multinationals; in the short run they are
aiding their potential long run competitors.) This long-
range development and the possible reactions by the Eastern
European socialist economies was discussed extensively during the annual meeting of Eastern European economists in

Budapest in June 1973. Gyorgy Adam, the Hungarian expert
on multinational corporations, summed up the conclusions
reached at the meeting in one of his papers presented to
Western audiences:

> In the context of the consideration of the inter-
> national competivity of socialist enterprises the
> role of American and non-U.S. based conglomerates
> and transnational corporations is considered very
> important. In view of their weight in the capi-
> talistic world economy serious thought is given
> to the establishment of socialist transnational
> corporations which may command an economic poten-
> tial sufficiently big to enable them to compete
> with the big Western corporations. Their estab-
> lishment is, of course, not merely a matter of
> organizational decisions: an adequate set of
> economic instruments is required to promote their
> birth and efficient operation.[15]

In this connection, it is worth mentioning that Yugoslavia
has already formed the first socialist multinational corporation. The firm, Energo-invest, is a "conglomerate
with 35 plants, six mines, a payroll of 25,000 and annual
sales of almost $200 million."[16] The March 1974 agree-
ment between the Soviet Union and the Federal Republic of
Germany concerning the search for opportunities to set up
joint companies in third countries with mixed Soviet-German
capital, management, and production indicates that under
the changing conditions, even the development of socialist-
capitalist multinational corporations is no longer an im-
possibility.

Multinational Sourcing

The worldwide operations of multinational corporations
can benefit Eastern European socialist economies through
the ability of such corporations to obtain their necessary
supplies from various parts of the globe. According to
the 1973 report of the United Nations on multinational
corporations, "Another characteristic of the very large
multinational corporations is their tendency to have a
sizable cluster of foreign branches and affiliates . . .
nearly 200 multinational corporations, among the largest
in the world, have affiliates in twenty or more countries."[17]
(See also Table 3.8.) While the most direct benefits of

such worldwide supplying networks are probably generated by multinational corporations that are engaged in equity joint ventures in the socialist economies, other types of close economic ties, such as contract manufacture and assembly operations, can also provide substantial multinational sourcing benefits.

The key to such benefits is the bilateral trade agreements that characterize most of the international trade relations of the Eastern European socialist economies. It is true that in 1971-72, the number of bilateral trade agreements between the socialist and Western European countries started to decline and that the European Economic Community Commission has decided to limit bilateral trade agreements between member countries and Eastern Europe. Nevertheless, enough bilateral trade agreements between Western and Eastern European and, most of all, between Eastern European and developing countries, exist to provide multinational sourcing benefits to the Eastern European economies. (See Table 3.2.)

Using their worldwide supply sources, multinational corporations can improve the trade relations of the Eastern European socialist economies by obtaining raw materials, parts, or finished products from a subsidiary or business partner located in a country with which the socialist economies have bilateral trade imbalances. The global sourcing ability of multinational corporations can also help the Eastern European socialist economies to avoid costly production bottlenecks, which even today plague many industrial firms throughout the region. While some of these problems are caused by domestic distribution inefficiencies, and could thus be prevented through a reorganization of distribution systems, others are generated by the uneven performance of socialist foreign trade enterprises that are responsible for the continuous flow of supplies from abroad.[18] The large-scale, worldwide suppliers of multinational corporations are less likely to create critical bottlenecks than the small-scale, and, at times, inexperienced socialist foreign trade enterprises, who frequently are limited in their choice of suppliers by political factors and trading regulations. In an era of increasing raw material scarcity and continually changing world-market prices such limitations can do incalculable damage to socialist industrial enterprises. On the other hand, multinational corporations are free and able to outbid most other firms in the scramble for high-priced raw materials and, thus, can assure a continuous flow of supplies to the socialist economies.

## Advanced Technology

The great demand of the Eastern European socialist economies for advanced technology is one of the major reasons for increased East-West trade. The new, intensive economic growth strategy is predicated on the more efficient utilization of resources that, in turn, is based on the availability of advanced technology. More specifically, the effects of advanced technology on the Eastern European socialist economies are primary and secondary. The primary effects show up in a relatively short period of time and consist of the development and manufacture of new products and the application of new production processes. The secondary effects take more time because industrial reorganization through mergers or separations and economies of scale through specialization involve the regrouping of resources.

Multinational corporations are the most important institutions involved in the international transfer of technology. Their vast capital and research and development resources as well as worldwide operations help not only the development but also the immediate application of advanced technology to the solution of everyday industrial problems. As a student of international transfer of technology put it:

> Increasingly the raison d'etre for most multinational companies is their superiority in science based or management technologies. Multinational companies can only penetrate a market or producing area if they can do something better than the local inhabitants. In some cases, a company may simply have low-cost funds, cheaper labor or special raw materials to exploit. But more and more, a multinational company's success depends on its superior management techniques, better product or manufacturing technologies, or operating economies of scale.[19]

The Eastern European socialist economies, however, are not interested in obtaining any kind of advanced technology. As a result of hard currency limitations, industrial organization problems, and occasionally because of the unavailability of required skills, advanced technology is obtained in a selective fashion within the framework of the overall national development goals. In the case of Hungary, for example, the selective infusion of advanced technology is currently directed chiefly toward the continued development of the chemical industry, especially the production and utilization of hydrocarbons, the aluminum industry, the manufacture of buses, and the manufacture and application of computers. Romania is eager to obtain advanced technology in oil exploration and refining in the production of petrochemicals, and in the manufacture of machine tools. Poland is particularly interested in advanced technology in the electronics and computer fields. It should be pointed out that in addition to individual national considerations, the CMEA "Complex Program" also influences decisions concerning the selective adoption of advanced technologies. The Eastern European socialist governments want to avoid costly duplication whenever possible. However, how the balance between individual national and collective CMEA interests is to be established is not clear.

It also needs to be pointed out that the Eastern European socialist governments insist on the continual updating of any technology obtained. As most of the major technological advancements are developed and applied by multinational corporations, it is understandable that the ability to update is one of the reasons that the Eastern European socialist economies prefer to obtain advanced technologies from such corporations.

The case of the Hungarian communications industry (telephones) has shown that the Eastern European socialist economies are also interested in medium-level technology as long as such technology is supportive of the selective industrial development goals as stated in the national plans. But, as pointed out before, the expression of such interest should not be interpreted by multinational corporations as an excellent opportunity to pass off dated technology.

The dominance of U.S. multinational corporations in some key industries, such as electronics and computers, somewhat limits the transfer of advanced technology to the socialist economies. This is so because U.S. multinationals are subject to the Export Administration Act controls upheld by the U.S. government. Although over the last few years the list of embargoed strategic items has been reduced, there are still enough advanced technology items on the list to create occasional problems for the Eastern Europeans. While in most cases such problems do not mean that the items in question cannot be obtained at all (other multinationals are glad to supply what U.S.-based corporations cannot), the possibly higher prices, and, most of all, delivery delays can lead to costly interruptions and postponements of important projects.[20] In the fall of 1973, for example, the Polish government was very anxious to close a $18 million deal with the U.S. Fairchild corporation to obtain integrated circuit technology, which is extensively used in modern weapons systems as well as in advanced computers. The final closing of the deal was continually delayed and finally rejected by the U.S. Department of Defense, which had reservations about providing such advanced technology to a socialist country. Despite similar reservations, in 1973 Westinghouse Electric concluded a $10 million turnkey contract for the construction of an advanced electronics plant near Warsaw, and Western Electric agreed to sell some $9 million worth of equipment and engineering services to extend the manufacturing capacity of Poland's electronics and semiconductor industry.

## Capital

The need of the Eastern European socialist economies for capital, especially in the form of long-term credits, is another compelling reason for closer economic ties with multinational corporations. Although some socialist countries—as, for example, Hungary—have been willing and able to raise substantial amounts in Western capital markets, most of the others try to secure inexpensive long-term credits through other means. The needs are pressing; according to a report of the Vienna Institute of Comparative Economics, for example, in 1973 Poland was $3 billion in debt to the West; Romania—$1.8 million; Bulgaria—$1.5 billion; and Czechoslovakia—$1 billion.[21] The switch from extensive to intensive economic growth strategy and the resulting demand for advanced technology, the continually increasing consumer expectations, and the asymmetrical nature of East-West trade are factors indicating that the need of the socialist economies for substantial additional credits from the West will continue to grow.

Attempts of the Eastern European socialist economies to secure the necessary credits at governmental levels have had varying success. France, Italy, the United Kingdom, and Japan, on the whole, went along with the desire of the socialist economies for low (about 6 percent during 1973-74) interest rate long-term credits. Their most important Western trading partner, the Federal Republic of Germany (1973 increase in trade, 41 percent), however, turned out to be far more exasperating to deal with than the others.[22] In spite of compelling foreign policy reasons to promote the "Ostpolitik" through economic means,

Chancellor Brandt found it very difficult to overcome the
objections of his economic and finance ministers who feared
the inflationary effects of large credits on the already
overheated domestic economy.  To make matters worse, Brandt's
successor, Chancellor Schmidt, is known to have strong
political and economic reservations about low-interest rate,
long-term credits to socialist Eastern Europe.

Table 3.6 presents data concerning the short-term financial assets and liabilities of major institutions in the
international money markets.  The dominant position of the
foreign subsidiaries of U.S.-based multinationals illustrates the financial power of multinational corporations
in general.

With their immense financial resources, multinational
corporations can in several ways help reduce the credit
pressures experienced by the Eastern European socialist
economies.  First, it is not inconceivable that under certain conditions multinationals can extend credit on their
own.  Second, multinational corporations can help raise
capital in Western capital markets.  Third, through their
worldwide operations, multinationals can perform switch-

TABLE 3.6

Estimated Short-Term Asset and Liability Positions of
Principal Institutions in International Money Markets,
1971
(billions of U.S. dollars)

| Institutions | Assets | Liabilities |
| --- | --- | --- |
| U.S. banks | 13.0 | 16.0 |
| U.S. nonbanks | 5.2 | 2.6 |
| Foreign banks | 52.7 | 46.5 |
| Foreign governments, central banks, and international organizations | 18.7 | n.a. |
| Foreign nonbanks | 6.8 | 11.4 |
| Foreign affiliates of U.S. corporations | 110.0 | 63.0 |
| Foreign branches of U.S. banks | 61.4 | 61.5 |
| Total | 267.8 | 201.0 |

Source:  U.S. Senate, Committee on Finance, The Multinational Corporations and the World Economy, February 26,
1973, p. 30.

trading operations on a considerably larger scale than any individual switch-trader or Western firm.[23] This can be especially important if doing business with an Eastern European socialist country involves counter-purchase requirements. Finally, through various types of industrial cooperation agreements, multinational corporations can contribute materials, equipment, technology, intermediary products, and parts. Whatever form the contribution takes, it can help decrease the credit pressures on the Eastern European socialist economies.

## Access to Markets

Among the numerous economic problems faced by the Eastern European socialist economies, one of the most critical is their limited access to markets. This is chiefly the result of the inability of most socialist industries to meet the product quality requirements of the highly competitive markets. According to the Polish publication Handel Zagraniczny, for example, "Progress in terms of quality products offered for marketing has not kept up with changes throughout the world. As a result of a decreasing capacity to compete, suppliers from CMEA countries have been relatively and, in some cases, absolutely eliminated from the international [consumer durables] market."[24] Table 3.7 presents the findings of a study conducted by the Czech economic weekly Hospodarske Noviny in three advanced Eastern European socialist economies, Czechoslovakia, Hungary, and Poland, concerning managerial views on how the quality of Eastern European products compares to that of Western European products.

As can be seen from this table, only in the case of metallurgy and food products do the managers of the three advanced Eastern European socialist countries believe that approximately one-third of their products can meet Western quality standards.

In addition to quality problems, the international marketing activities of most Eastern European foreign trade enterprises also leave much to be desired. Many enterprises, for example, continue to rely on foreign agents as their major distributors in the highly competitive Western markets. This leads to a loss of control over the marketing of products and, consequently, results in lower sales than could be achieved through a more appropriate market entry strategy, such as the creation of a marketing subsidiary or the joint marketing of products with a Western firm.

TABLE 3.7

Quality Comparison of Eastern and Western European Products by Czech, Hungarian, and Polish Managers
(percent)

| | Total Manufacturing | Metallurgy | Engineering | Chemicals | Consumer Goods | Food Products |
|---|---|---|---|---|---|---|
| Equal to highest Western standards | 24.3 | 33.8 | 17.9 | 27.8 | 26.0 | 31.3 |
| Meets about half Western standards | 36.7 | 35.9 | 39.5 | 40.3 | 34.4 | 29.7 |
| Meets few Western standards | 22.9 | 18.1 | 25.3 | 17.4 | 22.6 | 23.5 |
| Absolutely not in same class as Western products | 16.1 | 12.2 | 17.3 | 14.5 | 17.0 | 15.5 |

Source: <u>Business International Eastern European Report</u>, June 14, 1974, p. 186.

The switch from extensive to intensive growth and the
resulting economic reforms, together with the infusion of
advanced technology, were designed to gradually increase
industrial efficiency and, consequently, to improve the
quality of socialist products. The managerial development
programs, compulsory in all Eastern European socialist
countries, are expected to improve managerial performance
in general and international marketing activities in particular. On the other hand, the Eastern European governments
know very well that the carving out of long-run world
market-shares is a slow process requiring a great deal of
resources and effort. They also know that even under the
most favorable circumstances the risks associated with entering new markets are very high. Consequently, it is understandable that the Eastern European socialist economies
are very anxious to utilize the worldwide marketing networks of multinational corporations. Table 3.8 presents
data showing the percentage distribution of countries in
which multinational corporations maintain subsidiaries.
These data illustrate the scope of the marketing operations
of such corporations.

The worldwide marketing operations and strong market
positions held by large multinational corporations can help
the Eastern European socialist economies to reduce the high
cost and risk of international marketing operations. Given
appropriate economic incentives, multinational corporations
can be induced to participate in the joint global marketing
of products manufactured by the socialist economies to
world-market specifications under contractual arrangements
such as licensing. Or multinationals can engage in the
joint manufacture and worldwide marketing of dual trade-
mark products representing both multinational corporations
and the socialist economies. Whatever the arrangement,
the existing worldwide distribution systems, sophisticated
marketing expertise, and long-established reputation of
multinational corporations can help reduce the cost and
time involved in entering new markets for the socialist
economies, and, most of all, can help minimize the risk of
failures. This is very important because especially in
those product categories in which the Eastern Europeans
want to establish long-term market shares, such as machinery, chemicals, and transportation equipment, worldwide
competition is continually increasing. As pointed out before, the socialist governments are fully aware of this;
their position is that both technology and capital might
be difficult but not necessarily impossible to obtain in
the short run. The establishment of worldwide market

TABLE 3.8

Percentage Breakdown of Number of Subsidiaries, by Number
of Countries in Which Subsidiary's Parent System
Manufactured, for Various Categories of Subsidiaries

| Category of Subsidiary | Number of Countries in Which Subsidiary's Parent System Manufactured | | | | | |
|---|---|---|---|---|---|---|
| | 2 or 3 | 4 to 6 | 7 to 12 | 13 or More | Total Per- cent | Total Number |
| Non-U.S.-based systems (as of 1/1/71): | | | | | | |
| All subsidiaries | 20 | 16 | 28 | 36 | 100 | 13,541 |
| Manufacturing subsidi- aries | 19 | 16 | 29 | 36 | 100 | 5,511 |
| Sales subsidiaries | 18 | 19 | 25 | 38 | 100 | 3,267 |
| U.S.-based systems (as of 1/1/68): | | | | | | |
| All subsidiaries | 0 | 1.1 | 24 | 75 | 100 | 9,727 |
| Manufacturing subsidi- aries | 0 | 0.6 | 24 | 76 | 100 | 4,219 |
| Sales subsidiaries | 0 | 2.2 | 33 | 64 | 100 | 1,651 |
| World Subset of Systems (as of 1/1/68): | | | | | | |
| Non-U.S.-based sys- tems: | | | | | | |
| All subsidiaries | 0 | 0 | 23 | 77 | 100 | 6,153 |
| Manufacturing sub- sidiaries | 0 | 0 | 18 | 82 | 100 | 2,737 |
| Sales subsidiaries | 0 | 0 | 27 | 73 | 100 | 1,634 |
| U.S.-based systems: | | | | | | |
| All subsidiaries | 0 | 0 | 20 | 80 | 100 | 8,144 |
| Manufacturing sub- sidiaries | 0 | 0 | 19 | 81 | 100 | 3,334 |
| Sales subsidiaries | 0 | 0 | 28 | 72 | 100 | 1,309 |

Source: James W. Vaupel and Joan P. Curhan, The
World's Multinational Enterprises: A Sourcebook of Tables
(Boston: Graduate School of Business Administration, Har-
vard University, 1973), p. 468.

shares in highly competitive product categories, however, could easily take 5 to 10 years of concentrated efforts. Consequently, the worldwide marketing ability of multinational corporations is an extremely important benefit that closer economic ties with other types of Western firms could not provide. Hungarian economic officials, for example, have already indicated that in selecting multinational corporations for joint projects, marketing ability is in many cases the most important decision factor.

## Increased Industrial Efficiency

Most European socialist economies still suffer from low industrial efficiency caused by, among other things, dated technology, low labor discipline, poor industrial organization, and small domestic markets. The economic reforms were designed to eliminate the basic problems and to create an economic and managerial environment in which industrial efficiency can be improved. During the last couple of years progress was made; in most countries advanced technology and better labor discipline resulted in more efficient operations. Hungary, for example, has overcome the problem of high labor mobility during 1969-72, consequently labor productivity that was stagnating for some time finally increased.[25] The Hungarians have also attacked the problems of poor industrial organization. Until 1973-74 most industries were still dominated by large enterprises whose organizational structures and product lines were determined on the basis of past administrative considerations. Consequently, in 1972 for example, the 74 largest industrial enterprises produced 46 percent of total output, exported 61 percent of all exports, employed 34 percent of the total working population, but generated only 37 percent of all profits.[26] Understandably, inefficiency in such a large sector of the economy could not be tolerated any longer. On July 1, 1974 the first major move to reorganize the Hungarian economy along more efficient lines took place. The Red Star factory, one of the older industrial enterprises, ceased to exist as an independent enterprise and merged with the Raba Railway Carriage and Machine Works, one of the country's best managed and most efficient enterprises. Red Star also switched from the manufacture of tractors and dumpers to the manufacture of rear and front axles and other components necessary to produce buses for export. The merger and change in product line took place because Red Star's tractor production costs were considerably above international standards.

The small domestic markets, preventing specialization
and mass production, are a more difficult problem to tackle.
Although the CMEA "Complex Program" was developed, among
others, to provide each socialist country with a larger
market and consequently create opportunities for specialization, sales in such larger markets do not generate hard
currency and are continually hampered by bilateral trade
agreements.

Closer economic ties with multinational corporations
can indirectly or directly help the Eastern European socialist economies to speed up the process of improving industrial efficiency. Selling advanced technology and products to the socialist countries is perhaps the most indirect
form of such help. In a less indirect manner, multinational
corporations can, through joint marketing arrangements, in-
troduce the Eastern European economies to new markets and,
thus, create economic conditions under which specialization
and economies of scale in production can take place. In
addition, since such joint global marketing is possible
only if products are manufactured to world-market specifications, this can lead to more rational industrial organization, better labor discipline and better management.
Finally, through joint production and marketing multinational corporations can directly affect industrial efficiency. In addition to providing advanced technology and
better methods of industrial organization, such joint ventures also mean direct managerial involvement in all areas
of enterprise activity. While Eastern European managers,
on the whole, are an able and dedicated group, in certain
areas they lack the kind of insight that only years of experience can provide. As a result of past economic policies, socialist managers, for example, are weak in investment decision making. To illustrate the point, in 1974
the Czech newspaper Rude Pravo reported that in the Central Slovakia region $25.2 million worth of imported West-
ern machinery was standing unused in enterprise store-
rooms.[27] The newspaper emphasized that the machines were
unused because construction projects were not completed,
unexpected changes in projects called for different technologies, and because importers made mistakes in stating
technical specifications to Western suppliers. Through
close working relations, multinational managers can probably pass on a substantial part of both their skills and
experience in dealing with such issues.

## SELECTED ILLUSTRATIONS

While the number of large-scale long-term projects between multinational corporations and the Eastern European
socialist economies is still modest, the nature of the following selected ventures and the size, as well as reputation of the multinationals involved, serve as good illus-
trators of the type of relationships that are gradually
emerging.

In late 1972 the British subsidiary of Massey-Ferguson,
a Canadian-based multinational corporation, contracted a
production agreement with the Romanian Mecanoexport for the
manufacture of wheel-loaders.[28]  The contract also involved
technical aid to set up and manage the manufacturing operation as well as certain marketing rights and privileges.
Under the latter, for example, the Romanian company has
nonexclusive marketing rights for CMEA markets, but exclusive marketing rights for Romania.  Furthermore, the Romanian producer may also sell finished machines, manufactured under a licensing arrangement, to Massey-Ferguson,
which markets such machines through its worldwide distribution system.  Finally, subject to Massey-Ferguson's approval, the Romanians have the option to market their
products anywhere in the world.  Such approval is almost
automatic if the Romanian company wants to exercise its
option in soft-currency countries with which Romania has
bilateral trade agreements.

In 1973, the U.S. Control Data Corporation set up a
20-year joint venture, called Rom-Control Data, with Romania to produce and market printers, card punchers, and
other computer peripherals.[29]  Control Data owns 45 percent
of the venture with the Romanian Industrial Center for
Electronic and Vacuum Technology.  A very interesting feature of the contract is that in spite of minority position
Control Data has equal representation on the management
board.  The general manager is Romanian; his assistant and
the directors for production, engineering, and quality control are American.  U.S. employees are permitted to import
cars, furniture, refrigerators, and other items for per-
sonal use duty-free.  Their salaries are paid in U.S. dollars.  Control Data is marketing 85 percent of output
through its own distribution system while the remaining
15 percent are marketed by the Romanians in Romania and
third country markets in both East and West.  American ac-

counting methods are used, books are kept in U.S. dollars, and profits are divided according to equity ownership. To guarantee the inviolability of the venture, the Romanian State Council enacted the venture agreement into law and published the same in the Official Gazette.

The same year General Electric and the Romanian government signed an agreement that will lead to the establishment of projects in the electronics field involving various types of arrangements including an equity joint venture in Romania.[30] Dai-Nippon Ink & Chemicals, a Japanese multinational, accepted a 42.62 percent equity position in the Roniprot joint venture producing protein from hydrocarbons for use as animal feed also in Romania.[31] Finally, during late 1973 and early 1974 the Romanian government was exploring projects with, among others, Texas Instrument, General Tire & Rubber Company, and Pfizer, Inc. of the United States, and with several multinational chemical corporations from the Federal Republic of Germany. To investigate additional opportunities as they arise some 90 West German, British, and Japanese multinationals have already set up permanent offices in Bucharest. Particularly noteworthy are the Japanese efforts to establish themselves in Eastern Europe; by 1974 joint economic committees have been set up between Japanese businessmen and the Foreign Trade Chambers of Bulgaria, Czechoslovakia, the German Democratic Republic, Hungary, Poland, and Romania.

Other multinational corporations and socialist economies are also on the move. In 1972 Koehring of Milwaukee, a worldwide leader in the manufacture of construction equipment, signed a comprehensive venture agreement with Poland. By late 1973 the first manufactured products left the plant in Warsaw. The equipment bears the Koehring name with "Made by Warynski" underneath.[32] In November 1973 Honeywell of the United States signed its first venture agreement in Eastern Europe with Poland for the manufacture of automation systems for industrial production. The same year Western Electric (United States) contracted with the Polish Unitra to expand the manufacturing capacity of the Polish electronics and semiconductor industry through the construction and equipment of a new plant near Warsaw.[33] The agreement involved some $10 million.

Bowmar Canada, a wholly owned subsidiary of Bowmar Instruments Corporation USA, in 1973 contracted with the Hungarian electronic equipment producer Hiradastechnika for the establishment of a joint venture under the name Hirbow. The company is a trading company with the major objective to obtain the technology needed for the produc-

tion of calculators, to contract for their production in
Hungary, and to market the calculators in hard currency
markets and the CMEA region.  In the summer of 1974, Siemens of West Germany announced that it signed a contract
with the Hungarian company Intercoop for the establishment
of an equity-based joint venture.  The new company, called
Sicontact, was formed to prepare technological developments
(consulting engineering) in the electronics field and to
explore long-range joint venture possibilities between
Siemens and additional Hungarian enterprises.  Siemens
owns 49 percent, the Hungarian company 51 percent, of the
equity.  Management of the company is in the hands of a
mixed Hungarian-West German team.  Although the company is
in charge of service for all Siemens products throughout
Hungary, for the time being, it does not engage in any production.  The same year, Volvo of Sweden, the Hungarian
Csepel vehicle manufacturing enterprise, and Mogurt foreign
trade enterprise, formed an equity-based joint venture
called Volcom for the production and marketing of Lapplander
four-wheel drive automobiles.[34]  In addition to its basic
capital share, Volvo is also contributing machinery, tool-
ing, and licenses in the value of approximately U.S. $1
million.  Volvo has financial and operational control of
the venture and maintains ownership of the machines through
a leasing arrangement.  Finally, in 1974, Pepsico Inc.
(United States) announced that it signed an agreement to
bottle and market Pepsi-Cola in the German Democratic Republic thus considerably expanding the Eastern European
market for this American soft drink.  (Previous agreements
had been signed with Czechoslovakia, Hungary, Poland, and
Romania.)  This project has a special significance for the
future because it involved the perhaps most conservative
Eastern European socialist government and a U.S.-based multinational as well as a consumer product.

## SUMMARY

As a result of the political détente during the early
1970s East-West trade increased in both volume and scope.
By 1973 some 600 industrial cooperation agreements signaled
the beginning of a new era of economic relationships between the two worlds.

Early industrial cooperation, however, was marked by
the absence of large-scale long-term arrangements and by
a low participation rate of multinational corporations in
general, and U.S.-based multinationals in particular.  The

recognition by the Eastern European socialist governments that in the years to come multinational corporations are going to play an increasingly more important role in world trade led to the creation of economic conditions in the socialist economies that were designed to induce multinationals to increase their participation in East-West trade in general, and industrial cooperation in particular. Particularly important in this respect was the passage of joint venture laws permitting 49 percent equity ownership in Romania and Hungary.

The specific benefits of close economic ties between multinational corporations and the Eastern European socialist economies are considerable. Stable economic environments, lower production costs, skilled labor, and additional market opportunities on the one hand, and large-size technology, capital, and market control on the other, can help the Eastern European socialist economies to speed up their development process and enable multinational corporations to achieve long-term sales maximization in conjunction with risk aversion. Neither multinationals nor the Eastern European socialist economies could obtain similar overall gains through closer economic ties with other countries or other Western firms. The type of large-scale long-term projects that are gradually emerging indicate that this is understood and appreciated by both the multinationals and the Eastern European socialist economies. As for the details of such projects, Control Data's joint equity venture in Romania is a good illustration of the type of arrangements that can be worked out.

NOTES

1. UN Economic Commission for Europe, Analytical Report on Industrial Cooperation Among ECE Countries (E/ECE/844), March 14, 1973, pp. 3-4.
2. Ibid., p. 18.
3. United Nations, Secretariat and ST/ECA/190, Multinational Corporations in World Development (New York: United Nations, 1973), p. 41.
4. Jack Baranson, "Technology Transfer Through the International Firm," American Economic Review, May 1970, p. 438.
5. The Washington Post, November 11, 1973, p. M-6. For a general discussion of labor's position see International Labor Office, Multinational Enterprises and Social Policy (Geneva: ILO, 1973).

6. Business Week, March 9, 1974, p. 48.

7. Der Spiegel 28 (February 11, 1974): 48.

8. Business International Eastern European Report, August 10, 1973, p. 224.

9. Thomas A. Wolf, East-West Economic Relations and the Multinational Corporation (Washington, D.C.: Center for International Studies, 1973), p. 55.

10. Figyelo, October 24, 1973, p. 7.

11. Ibid.

12. Electronics Weekly, June 13, 1973, p. 17.

13. Figyelo, February 6, 1974, p. 2; and April 17, 1974, pp. 1-2.

14. Anthony Sampson, The Sovereign State of ITT (New York: Stein and Day, 1973), pp. 55-61.

15. Gyorgy Adam, "Problems of Inter-Firm Cooperation Between East and West," unpublished paper presented to the Third International Conference on Corporate Planning, Brussels, Belgium, September 17-19, 1973.

16. Business International Eastern Europe Report, November 17, 1972, p. 142.

17. United Nations, Secretariat and ST/ECA/190, op. cit., p. 7.

18. For an example of domestic supply distribution inefficiencies, see Geza Peter Lauter, The Manager and Economic Reform in Hungary (New York: Praeger, 1972), pp. 101-05.

19. James Brian Quinn, "Technology Transfer by Multinational Companies," Harvard Business Review, November-December 1969, p. 150.

20. For a study of the effects of the trade control legislation on U.S. East-West trade, see Thomas A. Wolf, U.S. East-West Trade Policy (Lexington, Mass.: D. C. Heath and Company, 1973).

21. Business International Eastern Europe Report, January 25, 1974, p. 18.

22. Die Zeit, March 8, 1974, p. 9.

23. For a discussion of switch-trading see Business International Eastern Europe Report, February 23 and March 9, 1973, pp. 51-52, 66-67.

24. Ibid., February 22, 1974, p. 52.

25. Lauter, op. cit., pp. 162-67.

26. Gazdasagi Kutato Intezet (Economic Research Institute), "A nagy ipari vallalatokrol" ("About Large Industrial Enterprises"), Gazdasag (Economics), December 1973, pp. 76-92.

27. Business International Eastern Europe Report, February 22, 1974, p. 56.

28. C. H. McMillan and D. P. St. Charles, _Joint Ventures in Eastern Europe: A Three-Country Comparison_ (Montreal: C. D. Howe Research Institute, 1973), pp. 37-43.

29. _Business International Eastern Europe Report_, April 20, 1973, p. 106; _Business Week_, December 1, 1973, pp. 40-43; and Hugh P. Donaghue, "Control Data's Joint Venture in Romania," _Columbia Journal of World Business_, December 1973, pp. 83-89.

30. _Business International Eastern Europe Report_, January 11, 1974, p. 14.

31. Ibid., February 8, 1973, p. 44.

32. Ibid., January 11, 1974, pp. 2-3.

33. Ibid., January 25, 1974, p. 30.

34. Chase World Information Corporation, _East-West Markets_, July 29, 1974, p. 6.

# 4

**PROBLEMS**

As shown in the previous chapter, close economic ties
between multinational corporations and the Eastern European
socialist economies can provide substantial economic benefits to both sides.  The realization of such benefits, however, is predicated on the mutually satisfactory handling
of several current and potential problems.  The following
is a discussion of such problems.

## GLOBAL POLITICAL UNCERTAINTY

While the increased participation of multinational
corporations in East-West industrial cooperation is partially a result of the détente between the United States
and the Soviet Union, it is important to keep in mind that
many of the global differences between the two major powers
still remain unresolved.  The presence of Soviet troops in
Eastern Europe and of the U.S. military in Western Europe,
as well as the continued existence of the Warsaw Pact and
NATO Alliance, are issues that can easily erupt into misunderstandings and, consequently, destroy the fragile economic bridges that were built so carefully during the last
few years.  It is true that some socialist countries, as,
for example, Romania, conduct a relatively independent
foreign policy and, thus, are perhaps less affected by
changing relationships between the superpowers.  This does
not mean, however, that if U.S.-Soviet relations took an
unexpected turn for the worse, Romania could be neutral.
The same holds true for the Western European countries and
Japan, who rely on the United States for military protection.

It is important to explain that the political uncertainty discussed here refers to the fundamental political
relationship between the capitalist and socialist worlds
and does not negate the argument presented in Chapter 3
that multinational corporations are more independent of
national governments than nonmultinationals. The point
is that while multinational corporations are relatively
free of national loyalties, they do not exist in a political
vacuum and, consequently, are influenced by the kind of
global political developments that make up the détente.

Political uncertainty is one of the reasons that
numerous multinational corporations are still somewhat
cautious about signing large-scale long-term agreements
with the Eastern European socialist economies, who, for
developmental reasons, are far more interested in such
agreements than smaller short-term deals. Although some
socialist governments, such as the Romanian and Hungarian,
are offering multinationals strong incentives to participate in large-scale, long-term projects (for example, the
enactment of equity joint ventures into laws and the ap-
pointment of National Banks as guarantors), many multinational corporations are still concerned about getting
caught by sudden political changes. Without doubting the
sincerity of the U.S. and Soviet, as well as of the Romanian
and Hungarian governments, such concern is not entirely
unfounded. The détente is only a few years old and many
of its details have not yet been worked out; it is thus
reversible. One can only hope that some day this will no
longer be the case. Until then, the cautious posture of
many multinationals is understandable.

The case of the U.S.-based multinationals merits a
few special observations. As long as the U.S. government
and Congress continue to use the MFN clause and the Export
Administration Act as political weapons, and as long as
the subsidiaries of U.S.-based multinationals are subject
to strict governmental controls limiting their economic
relations with the socialist countries, such corporations
are bound to exhibit even more reluctance than their Western European and Japanese counterparts.[1] Such U.S. policies naturally also negatively affect the behavior of the
Eastern European socialist economies toward U.S.-based
multinationals, although both the technology and management know-how of these multinationals is in great demand
throughout the region.

Close economic ties between multinational corporations and the Eastern European socialist economies are also impeded by mutual distrust. This distrust is more than just the usual reservation newly acquainted business partners display, and is partially a result of the previously discussed political uncertainty and partially the consequence of 10 to 15 years of hostile propaganda experienced in both East and West during the cold war years. Over the last decade, conditions of course have changed. Nevertheless, it is still not easy for both the multinationals and the Eastern European socialist governments to trust each other. Despite the détente, multinationals continue to see in the socialist governments regimes whose ideology calls for the elimination of capitalism. On the other hand, ideologically the Eastern European socialist governments see multinational corporations as the epitome of profit-maximizing capitalist business empires. As illustrated in Chapters 2 and 3, for pragmatic reasons the socialist governments have developed more favorable views on multinationals, and both the socialist governments and multinational corporations have recognized that closer economic ties can gener—ate substantial economic benefits that neither could obtain through closer relations with other firms or countries. Consequently, the emerging economic relationships are handled very pragmatically. Such pragmatism, however, does not mean that all real or imagined reasons for mutual distrust have been eliminated or forgotten.

Close economic ties with multinational corporations assume more open Eastern European societies. This necessity appears to fuel the distrust of the socialist governments who fear that close ties can increase the incidence of economic-industrial spying. Because most socialist governments are vague about what information they consider classified and because closer economic ties can only be developed--see the UN Commission for Europe report--if valid and reliable information is available, multinational corporations can easily be accused of engaging in economic-industrial espionage when in fact they are only collecting data that is necessary to conduct their business. The Warsaw newspaper Express Wieczorny reported a case in point in 1974.[2]

The West German representative of Linde Ag in Poland and a Polish engineer had been arrested on the charge of "economic espionage" for the collection of information on how much Polish foreign trade enterprises were willing to

pay for petrochemical installations sold, among others, by
Linde Ag.  It was also alleged that the Polish engineer,
in exchange for small gifts, passed on information concerning certain improvements the Poles made on imported petrochemical equipment.  As a result of these developments,
the Polish press started a campaign to warn officials and
workers about the dangers of Western "economic espionage."
Prawo i Zycie, the lawyers' weekly, for example, discussed
the Linde Ag case in detail and pointed out the various
mistakes the Polish engineer made in underestimating the
"devious" designs of the West German firm.  It is interesting to note that a representative of the Polish firm, for
which the arrested Polish engineer worked, maintained publicly that Linde Ag helped build the petrochemical plants
in Poland and that the West Germans also provided most of
the technical know-how.  Furthermore, the official argued,
it is common practice all over the world to provide business
partners with small gifts and that such gifts are not necessarily a payment for the passing on of information.

Industrial espionage, of course, is part of today's
highly competitive global economic scene.  Consequently,
in fairness to the socialist governments it has to be
pointed out that some multinational representatives and
managers may very well be involved in such activities.  In
March 1974, for example, the New York Times published the
following on its editorial page:

> The American businessman active in trade and in-
> vestment matters in such politically sensitive
> listening posts as Hong Kong and Vienna may be
> --shhh--an American spy.
>       That's not exactly news to the natives, who
> have developed a sharp eye for the American--or
> for that matter, English, Russian or any other--
> espionage agent, but it's unusual for the spy
> industry's home office to let out statistics on
> this aspect of its work, as an unnamed official
> in Washington did recently.
>       . . . There are more than 200 American in-
> telligence agents stationed abroad posing as
> businessmen.  Some are full-time operatives,
> and the business concerns that provide for their
> "cover" receive payments from the United States
> Government to help defray business overhead.
> Others are part-timers.[3]

In spite of such evidence, some Eastern European socialist governments may be overreacting. Statements, such as the one made by the Polish paper, _Polityka_, that "economic espionage is a permanent interest of the Western press. . . . This penetration could grow as the Polish role in the international markets increases. . . . If we want to compete against our economic rivals, we cannot permit ourselves to neglect the problem"--are not going to help reduce the distrust.[4] The 1971 Romanian codification of control over "state secrets"--while very rigid in nature --might be a more workable solution than the publication of vague and threatening statements. According to the code, Romanian citizens have to follow detailed procedures in giving information to foreigners, all interviews by foreigners require special permission, foreigners cannot enter industrial areas other than administrative offices and exhibits without special permission, and, finally, foreigners who are permitted to visit industrial areas must wear special badges.[5] The Czechs, it appears, have also considered the problem. The economic weekly, _Hospodarske Noviny_, for example, published an article in 1973 referring to the "hundreds of training courses, briefing sessions, discussion evenings, and instruction classes that had been conducted for persons who deal with state, economic and official secrets."[6]

The previously mentioned UN Economic Commission for Europe Report also found the lack of reliable information as one of the major problems impeding East-West industrial cooperation. The commission's findings are applicable to the emerging relationship between multinational corporations and the Eastern European socialist economies:

> A more widespread and accurate knowledge of opportunities for negotiating and concluding industrial co-operation contracts and of the institutional framework to which such contracts must necessarily be adapted would seem to be a primary requirement for the further development of this type of business partnership.
>
> In the past, the information base which gave rise to such contracts has tended to be somewhat narrow and haphazard. In many, and probably most, cases contracts appear to have been negotiated and concluded between partners who already had a long-standing and close business relationship or

series of contacts or who had already been active in east-west trade; thus, industrial co-operation was essentially an outgrowth of these existing links. In these cases, also, it was mainly the larger enterprise which participated. Only in relatively few cases were such contracts reached between partners who had no previous east-west trade links and who had been brought together as a result of the international diffusion of information about specific opportunities for industrial co-operation.

. . . The second aspect of the information problem is the need for a more widespread and accurate knowledge of the institutional framework in which industrial co-operation contracts must be negotiated, concluded and applied. The basic differences in economic systems and which are reflected in differences in methods of business management and decision-making must be taken fully into account when considering, drawing up, and implementing such contracts. In this connexion it is of primary importance to bear in mind the differences which exist especially with respect to the authority for and levels of decision-making. . . . In the centrally planned economies industrial co-operation contracts must be fitted into a national plan which is a basic law and framework for decision-making for the country as a whole and for its constituent parts; in the market economies, such contracts can be generally made and carried out at the sole discretion of the enterprise concerned, even though there may be a certain degree of final control exercised by the Government. A wider knowledge of the decision-making process in each of the systems and in each country concerned is a prerequisite for the further development of industrial co-operation.[7]

The report recognized that information problems also exist at the "technical" level of cooperation:

It is also important to take into account the differences which exist with respect to information on new technologies, techniques and "know-how." In the centrally planned economies, such information is centralized and is made available

to enterprises in order to achieve the objectives
of the plan, whereas in the market economies such
information is [in general] privately owned and
its diffusion is not governmentally organized.
In addition, of course, there is an informational
problem inherent in any industrial co-operation
contract involving "know-how": it is often necessary for the seller to provide enough information to the buyer so that the value of the trans-
action can be appreciated while not providing so
much that the buyer would lose interest in con-
cluding a contract which would oblige him to pay
for information already obtained that is sufficient to fill his needs.[8]

Finally, the UN commission emphasized that certain
favorable developments might reduce the problem in the
future:

Some steps have already been taken to circulate
internationally information about industrial cooperation opportunities and about the relevant
institutional frameworks. Thus, for example, the
joint commissions established under intergovern-
mental agreements on trade, science, technology
and industrial co-operation have been an important means of transmitting information of this
kind. The foreign commerce departments of Governments also have acted as transmitter of a
considerable amount of information either on special request or in periodical publications. Certain international business information services
also devote special attention to industrial co-operation in the east-west context. Furthermore,
the ECE has contributed--particularly through the
discussions on industrial co-operation which have
taken place in the Commission and the Committee on
the Development of Trade, as well as through its
research studies and its Meeting of Experts on Industrial Co-operation held in 1972--to the international diffusion of knowledge on this subject.[9]

There are no easy solutions to this problem. However,
as the number of large-scale, long-term projects--such as
equity joint ventures--in socialist Eastern Europe increases, the socialist governments and multinational corporations have to work out an agreement as to what consti-

tutes "economic-industrial spying" and what is "the collection of necessary economic and industrial information." In addition, they probably also have to identify the difference between "economic-industrial spying," which has only industrial significance, and "economic-industrial spying," which also has military implications. While this is not easy to do, it has to be attempted, because someday for some multinational representative or manager, it might mean the difference between a relatively straightforward civil legal procedure and a rather involved process conducted by military tribunals.

The lack of trust on the part of multinational corporations manifests itself chiefly in the reservations multinationals have about the inviolability and enforcement of legal contracts in the Eastern European socialist economies. This does not mean that they have reason to believe that the Eastern Europeans do not live up to their contractual obligations; on the contrary, the performance of the socialist economies under regular trade contracts has been exemplary. However, the increasingly more complex nature of East-West economic relations (that is, equity and other types of joint ventures) has added a new, uncertain dimension to the issue. Especially important in this respect are the many unknown and untested details concerning the rights and responsibilities of the participants. Although, for example, Control Data's pioneering venture with the Romanians gives an indication of what can be expected, not enough time has passed to evaluate the detailed consequences and implications of the contract. A case in point of what can happen is the experience of the West German BASF multinational corporation, which, through one of its subsidiaries, contracted with the German Democratic Republic to build two plants and to sell 19 licenses for a total of 63 million West German marks.[10] Because certain things went wrong in the plants, the East Germans refused payment for the work, and most important, also refused to let the West Germans eliminate the problems. For the licenses they paid only half the price.

Another aspect of the issue is the concern of multinational corporations that, after signing of large-scale, long-term contracts, the socialist governments might pass new laws and issue new rules that might negatively effect their rights and responsibilities. This is an important concern because--as mentioned before--the socialist economies are far more interested in signing long-term (5 to 20 years) than short-term contracts, and, consequently, are doing everything possible to induce multinationals to

participate in such contracts. Although in the case of
Control Data the Romanian government enacted the venture
into law and appointed its National Bank as a guarantor,
thus reducing the danger of such a development, there are
cases when foreign companies suddenly found themselves in
such an undesirable situation. The experience of the Austrian vehicle manufacturing company, Steyr-Daimler-Puch,
serves as a good example. Steyr-Daimler-Puch signed a
five-year coproduction agreement with the Hungarian tractor
manufacturing enterprise Red Star in 1968.[11] As discussed
in the previous chapter, because of industrial reorganization, Red Star was merged with another Hungarian enterprise
and its production line was also changed during 1974. The
decision to do so, naturally, was reached much sooner and,
thus, the Austrian company was informed before the expiration of the contract that Red Star is no longer going to
produce the required components for the joint product. It
is important to point out that the Hungarian decision was
not made with malice, the intent was not to damage the
Austrian company, but to reorganize Hungarian industry in
a more efficient manner. The Austrian company was not
seriously damaged because during the early stages it
noticed that the coproduction process did not work too well
and, consequently, prepared itself for the eventual disso-
lution of the contract through the development of a substi-
tute product for the coproduced one. Nevertheless, such
occurrences influence multinational corporations who are
requested to consider large-scale, long-term ventures in
the Eastern European socialist economies.

The UN Economic Commission for Europe also discussed
the lack of a consistent and enforceable international
legal framework as one of the problems interfering with
the expansion of East-West industrial cooperation. The
commission's observations are relevant to the emerging relationship between multinationals and the socialist economies:

> International contracts for industrial co-opera-
> tion may raise juridical and related problems
> which, if left unsolved, can prevent a maximal
> development of this form of economic co-opera-
> tion. A more certain legal framework for such
> contracts, based firmly in national legislation
> and international conventions or codes of prac-
> tice, could undoubtedly encourage the further
> growth of industrial co-operation. In some ECE
> countries special legislation of this kind is

being prepared. The recent lack of international norms which would provide a generally accepted basis for such contracts would appear to act as a constraint on the full development of industrial co-operation.[12]

Finally, multinational corporations are also concerned that as a result of unexpected political and economic developments their large-scale, long-term ventures, especially those based on equity participation, could be taken over by the socialist governments. As mentioned before, the performance of the Eastern Europeans under the current trade and cooperation contracts has not given multinationals any reason to believe that this could happen. On the contrary, the enactment of equity joint ventures into laws, the various other types of guarantees offered, and the increasing involvement of the socialist economies with ventures in the West, indicate that such a concern is currently unfounded. However, multinational corporations have had bad experiences in the past. A 1968 study, for example, reported that since World War I, 187 U.S. companies were involved in 240 acts of expropriation, 171 of these in socialist countries (137 in Cuba alone).[13] Another 1969 study found that during the 1946-68 era, 41 British and 14 American companies (together with 110 seizures of insurance firms) were expropriated in 13 different countries.[14] Since quite a few of the companies involved were multinational, it is understandable that in spite of the positive current evidence, multinational corporations are concerned.

## INFLEXIBILITY OF SOCIALIST ECONOMIC AND ADMINISTRATIVE STRUCTURES

The major economic and administrative characteristics --extensively discussed in the literature--of the Eastern European socialist economies also tend to interfere with the development of closer economic ties with multinational corporations.[15] Although during the late 1960s and early 1970s every socialist economy had been reformed to some degree, the structural and administrative changes introduced did not go far enough to eliminate all the rigid features of past systems. Even under Hungary's New Economic Mechanism, the most liberal Eastern European reform, the overall planning, coordination, and expansion of the national economy continues to be uneven. Moreover, as discussed in Chapter 2, the inefficient intra-CMEA trading practices help perpetuate many of the rigid economic features throughout the entire region.

Consequently, multinational corporations seeking closer economic ties with the Eastern European countries encounter several problems. First, the planned nature of all socialist economies, and especially, the selective industrial development programs set strict limits to the type of activities multinationals can get involved in. Romanian President Ceausescu's statement concerning the place of joint ventures in his country summed up the Eastern European investment policy very well:

> The setting up of joint companies which presupposes foreign investments in Romania, is linked to the program of development of Romanian industry. As such, their number and size will be in conformity with the areas in which we consider them necessary and in which, of course, we also find partners interested in participating.[16]

While each socialist economy has its own priorities, most current programs call for the development of industrial sectors, more specifically for the development of the electronic, machine-building, transportation, chemical, and oil-refining industries. In addition, the activities of multinationals must also fit the national, industrial, and--if trade is involved--foreign trade plans in terms of the resources used (raw materials, labor) and the output contributed. This can become especially complicated if activities of multinational corporations are spread over several industries. Because most of the projects multinationals are invited to participate in are large-scale and long-term, this is usually the case.

The administrative mechanisms set up in the socialist economies to deal with these issues are complex and slow-moving. Decision-making authority for major projects is highly centralized and information systems are sluggish; as a result project negotiations can involve an inordinate amount of time.[17] As pointed out before, the more industries are involved in the project the more pronounced this problem tends to become. The Eastern European governments are aware of this difficulty and, as much as possible, are trying to improve the situations. New, special agencies are set up to explore and negotiate projects. To more effectively channel information and, thus, to accelerate negotiations, authority relationships are clarified and, in some cases, simplified. While there can be no doubt

about the sincerity of these efforts, it seems that they
are designed to treat symptoms and not the root cause of
the problems: the planned and centrally directed nature
of the socialist economies.

The complexity and sluggishness of administrative
mechanisms can become a problem for multinational corporations even after the project contracts have been signed.
If, for example, as a result of technological and economic
developments, conditions in world markets change over time,
the adjustment of contractually agreed upon procedures, such
as the production process and competitive behavior, cannot
be swiftly implemented. Because multinationals are asked
to participate in large-scale, long-term projects that must
be incorporated in national and sectoral plans, and that
are spread over several industries, such adjustments auto-
matically involve several layers of complex and slow-moving
governmental bureaucracy. The adjustment process can become especially prolonged if specialization-based subcontractors are also participating in the project. Eastern
European government bureaucrats and industrial managers
have very limited experience in the coordination of subcontractors, because until very recently, each industry
produced all the components it needed to manufacture the
final product. A West German engineering firm also found
that Eastern European subcontractors do not attach as much
importance to meeting obligations in their own countries
than they do to the meeting of export commitments; this,
despite the fact that the domestic customer may be a Western firm paying in hard currency.[18]  As before, the socialist governments are fully aware of these difficulties. Administrative relationships are simplified, and managers
are carefully trained to handle the increased decision-
making authority delegated to them. In Bulgaria, for example, Western firms with financial interests in Bulgarian
enterprises are, in some cases, allowed to oversee production and quality control, although, officially, equity
joint ventures are not yet permitted. It must be pointed
out, however, that in general the changes and allowances
do not go far enough to result in substantial improvements
in the near future.


OWNERSHIP STRATEGIES OF
MULTINATIONAL CORPORATIONS

A study of joint venture potentials in socialist Eastern Europe concluded the following:

In addition to the pronounced trend toward cooperation agreements, during 1971 the possibility for Western firms to participate in joint ventures inside Eastern Europe became a reality. In this work, we have analyzed, in detail the prospects for these joint ventures (advantages versus disadvantages) and have concluded that, at this time, every potential motivation for a joint-venture could be satisfied through some form of nonequity cooperation arrangement.[19]

While the findings of this study are valid, the past ownership strategies of multinational corporations in general and of the U.S.-based multinationals in particular indicate that in formulating their Eastern European strategies most multinationals are not likely to pay much attention to such arguments. A 1971 study, for example, reported that during the 1960-70 period 60 percent of new U.S. subsidiaries established overseas were fully owned, in 8 to 9 percent of the cases the U.S. corporations had majority ownership positions.[20] Although as reported by another study, relative to U.S.-based multinationals the Japanese appear to be more willing to take minority positions (in the cases studied 37 percent were minority positions, 34 percent majority, and 29 percent wholly owned subsidiaries), the ownership strategies of even the most flexible Japanese multinationals were based on a degree of equity participation.[21]

According to Richard D. Robinson,[22] the theoretical determinants on which international ownership strategies should be based are:

> Competitive position
> Availability of acceptable associates
> Legal constraints
> Control requirements
> Benefit/cost relationship

While Robinson's theoretical framework is logical and comprehensive, concerning its use by multinational corporations, he made the following observation:

> It is clear, on the basis of fairly intensive research, that exceedingly few corporations make a conscious, deliberate cost/benefit analysis of a proposed overseas operation for the purpose of determining the most profitable relationship--for

example, 100 percent ownership, some degree of joint ownership, contract plus some degree of ownership, or entirely contractual.

. . . A 15-country survey of international mixed ventures failed to turn up a situation in which the private firm appeared to have made a careful cost/benefit analysis of the possible relationships so as to determine which would be most profitable. Rather, the arrangements that emerged were simply the result of a bargaining process, the outcome of which was based on the perceived relative power position of the two parties at a particular point in time.[23]

In other words, not only do multinational corporations, especially U.S.-based ones, aim for full ownership--or at least some form of majority equity participation--but in deciding between the different ownership strategies in most cases they do not even engage in a cost-benefit analysis of the alternatives available. For practical purposes, the strategies of most multinational corporations are based on the desire to obtain maximum ownership under a given set of circumstances, because they equate ownership with control.

Robinson pointed out that in their drive for maximum ownership, multinational corporations are motivated by the desire to obtain control and thus to avoid conflicts with foreign partners in a host of operational areas (to be discussed later) such as dividend policy, plant expansion, and market penetration.[24] Empirical evidence supports this contention. The UN study of multinationals--quoted in Chapter 3--concluded that multinational corporations aim for maximum ownership, or at least, for some form of equity participation to avoid conflicts in areas that are vital to the accomplishment of their long-range objectives.[25]

The Eastern European ownership strategy of multinational corporations is consistent with their strategy in the rest of the world. Although as reported by the UN Commission for Europe, some 600 East-West industrial agreements were signed by 1973, large-scale, long-term projects, such as the Control Data project in Romania, were developed only after the Romanian government permitted foreign equity participation. Other major projects, such as the Volvo deal in Hungary, became a reality only after the Hungarian government decided to extend similar privileges to foreign partners. The Bulgarian magazine Novo Vreme reported that Western corporations want "equal or majority ownership of enterprises in Bulgaria and the transfer of profits in convertible currencies without restrictions."[26] (The magazine also pointed out that this is a major factor holding back increased Bulgarian industrial cooperation with the West.)

The passing of equity-based joint venture laws in Romania and Hungary indicates that the governments of these two socialist countries are not only aware of the ownership strategies of multinational corporations but also have acknowledged the necessity that to induce multinationals to participate in large-scale, long-term projects, they must meet, at least, their minimum ownership expectations. As President Ceausescu of Romania put it:

> We consider that joint companies are more advantageous than the forms of loan we used and are still using. It is a greater incentive also for the foreign companies in ensuring the delivery of advanced technologies, in pursuing the maintenance of a high rate of production, in realizing corresponding profits for the joint company, too. As you see, the reasons are quite pragmatic: the wish to attain a faster development of industry, ensuring at the same time corresponding benefits to the companies we are to cooperate with.[27]

On the other hand, the governments of Bulgaria, Czechoslovakia, the German Democratic Republic, and, to some extent, Poland continue to display a more reserved attitude than the Romanians or Hungarians. Although the Pepsi-Cola project in the German Democratic Republic is an indication of a gradually changing attitude toward multinationals, the nonequity nature of the project is strictly in line with the current thinking of the more reserved socialist governments.

The general framework of the Romanian and Hungarian joint venture laws (see Appendix A for the Hungarian one) is reasonably clear-cut. Foreign equity ownership is limited to 49 percent and the foreign partner's share is formally guaranteed by the governments. The numerous technical details of joint ventures, such as the operating policies and distribution of managerial authority, both the Romanians and Hungarians prefer to work out on a case-by-case basis. Control Data Corporation's venture is a good example of the kind of arrangements that can be worked out in Romania and perhaps even in Hungary.

The Polish situation is less clear.  Although equity
joint ventures are permitted, it appears that the Polish
government prefers to work out not only the technical details on a case-by-case basis but also not to provide a
legal framework similar to the ones the Romanians and Hungarians provided.  In a speech, made during his visit to
the United States in October 1974, the First Secretary of
the Polish Communist Party, Edward Gierek, confirmed this:

> Here, I should like to say that we are indeed pre-
> pared to consider various forms of cooperation in
> industry, as well as in joint trade-promotion that
> would include third markets.  Poland's legislation
> provides for a broad framework for these kinds of
> ventures and there is no need to introduce any new
> laws.  We are approaching these matters in a prag-
> matic way, aware both of the real advantages that
> individual projects can produce and the specific
> requirements for their implementation.  We shall
> always be ready to give serious consideration to
> any serious proposal.[28]

Thus, in spite of the acknowledged desirability of
closer economic ties with multinational corporations and
the existence of equity joint venture laws in two countries,
the Eastern European socialist governments in general set
very strict limits to the ownership strategies of multinationals.  Even under the best of conditions, such as in
Romania and Hungary, the most multinationals can get is an
equity-based minority position.  Of course, it is possible
that through the various technical details of ventures,
multinational corporations can maintain adequate control
over the major activities, such as quality control and marketing, that effect their long-range objectives.  However,
since these vital details have to be negotiated on a case-
by-case basis, many multinationals may have reservations
about participating in large-scale, long-term projects,
because not enough examples of such arrangements exist and
because in the socialist countries during negotiations the
relative power positions may not--as in most other parts
of the world--be in their favor.


## INCOMPATIBILITY OF OBJECTIVES

As discussed in Chapter 3, closer economic ties between multinational corporations and the Eastern European

TABLE 4.1

Potential Benefits of Closer Economic Ties Between
MNCs and Socialist Economies

| Benefits to Multina-<br>tional Corporations | Benefits to the Eastern<br>European Socialist Economies |
|---|---|
| Stable political and<br>economic conditions | Relative political independence |
| | Size |
| Stability and quality<br>of labor | Multinational sourcing |
| | Advanced technology |
| Lower production costs | |
| | Capital |
| New markets | |
| | Access to markets |
| New technology | Increased industrial efficiency |

socialist economies can generate a host of benefits for
both parties.  Table 4.1 presents a summary of these potential benefits.

The possible mutuality of interests based on these
different benefits, however, does not necessarily mean
that the specific joint venture objectives of multinationals and of the socialist economies are always fully
compatible.

The benefit of lower production costs to multinational
corporations, for example, is predicated on the availability of skilled low-wage labor in the socialist economies
and on the setting up of joint ventures in Eastern Europe
that manufacture labor-intensive products.  The socialist
economies, however, do not face any unemployment problems
and, most of all, are far more interested in obtaining advanced technology, that is, production methods that are
not labor but capital intensive.  This possible conflict
of joint venture objectives is even more pronounced in
those countries, as, for example, Hungary and Czechoslovakia, where in several industries, such as machine-building, a gradual shortage of skilled metal-cutters, welders,
and fitters has developed.[29]

Additional conflicts between joint venture objectives can develop in the technology transfer and marketing areas. As pointed out before, the socialist economies are chiefly interested in advanced technologies while, in many cases, multinational corporations might enter an Eastern European joint venture to extend the life cycle of existing products or to utilize medium-level technology. This can be especially true if multinationals want to enter markets in developing countries with whom the Eastern Europeans maintain bilateral trade agreements. In the marketing field, the major concern of the socialist economies is the establishment of permanent market-shares in the hard currency areas of the world. Multinational corporations, however, may want to reserve those markets to themselves and consider an Eastern European venture as a vehicle only to enter other socialist and developing economies.

Finally, as mentioned many times before, the Eastern European socialist economies prefer multinationals to participate in large-scale, long-term projects. The socialist governments believe, justifiably, that only through such projects can they obtain the benefits that closer economic ties with multinational corporations provide. On the other hand, multinationals may be very concerned about the loss of flexibility in large-scale, long-term projects, and, consequently, may shy away from 15- to 20-year deals.

It could be argued that such potential conflicts between multinational corporations and the Eastern European socialist economies should be identified and explored during the negotiation stages. While there is an element of truth in this argument, it ignores certain realities of both the capitalist and socialist world of business. First, while both the multinationals and the socialist economies have a set of clear-cut objectives that they are willing to state publicly, in almost every case they also have additional objectives that they keep secret for strategic reasons during both the negotiations and implementation stage of a project. Moreover, as the political, economic, and social environment in both the capitalist and socialist world changes, multinationals and their socialist venture partners might be influenced by a fundamentally different set of changing variables. Consequently, the frequency and magnitude of potential conflicts is multiplied, because while they both want to continue to benefit from a joint venture in equal proportions, they might have to do so in continually changing, and thus, essentially unpredictable ways.

# INCOMPATIBILITY OF OPERATIONAL
## POLICIES AND PROCEDURES

Closely related to conflicts caused by a differing set of joint venture objectives are potential conflicts generated by differing views on operational policies and procedures. Richard D. Robinson identified the following areas in which joint venture partners can hold differing policy and procedural views:

1. ownership--the sale or transfer of equity to third parties;
2. dividend policy--distribution versus investment;
3. borrowing--acceptable debt/equity ratios;
4. plant expansion--what and where;
5. research and development--level, purpose, location;
6. production processes--degree of integration, degree of capital-labor intensity;
7. source of supply--external or internal, transfer prices;
8. quality standards--domestic or absolute, international standards;
9. product mix--diversification, competitive exports;
10. reinvestment--dilution of equity held by a minority;
11. terms of sales--credit, servicing, pricing;
12. market area--restricted or open;
13. market penetration--choice of channels, promotional effort;
14. labor-management relations--degree of paternalism, union recognition and negotiation, national versus international negotiation, levels of remuneration, profit-sharing;
15. management selection and remuneration--nationality, skills required, number, salaries, decision-making style (degree of participation, calculation, and formalization);
16. political--honesty, company-government relations, degree of sensitivity to political decisions (for example, regarding desired allocation of national resources);
17. image projected[30]

Because of the special nature of the relationship between multinational corporations and the Eastern European socialist economies, not all of these problem areas are relevant.

For example, dividend policies, borrowing, and company-government relations are issues that multinationals and their Eastern European partners probably would not have to face. On the other hand, several of the other areas, such as plant expansion, quality standards and choice of distribution channels are critical operational areas in which misunderstandings are bound to occur.

As before, it could be argued that potential policy and procedural conflict areas should be identified and explored during the negotiation stages. This is a reasonable position to take and many of the operational policies and procedures are in fact agreed upon prior to implementing joint ventures. However, the passage of time and the changing environment has the same effect on policies and procedures that it has on organizational objectives. As a consequence, both the multinationals and their socialist partners might be subject to a different set of pressures that might make the coordination of policies and procedures an extremely difficult process.

## ABSENCE OF SPECIAL TRADE REGULATIONS

The UN Commission Report also emphasized that the lack of special treatment for goods produced under East-West industrial cooperation contracts can have a limiting effect on the expansion of such cooperation. This problem can also slow down the development of closer ties between multinationals and the socialist economies:

> While industrial co-operation has helped to provide practical ways of overcoming certain barriers to trade, the further growth of this form of co-operation could undoubtedly be promoted if it were possible to provide special treatment in respect of trade regulations for goods covered by industrial co-operation contracts. It is recognized that the problem is a complex one, and that it raises issues which go beyond industrial co-operation as such. But measures of this kind aimed specifically at encouraging industrial co-operation would seem to deserve renewed consideration at the present time, when ECE Governments are making efforts to increase east-west trade far beyond the levels achieved in the past and to bring about a new era of improved economic relations between countries having different systems.[31]

113

## LIMITED FINANCING

Another problem the UN report found to interfere with the expansion of East-West industrial cooperation is limited financing.  As before, this is a problem that can easily interfere with the emerging relationship between multinationals and the Eastern European socialist economies:

> East-West industrial co-operation develops in a context of financial constraint--due to limitations on trading possibilities, balance-of-payments difficulties, etc.  Industrial co-operation contracts therefore frequently provide that payment for machinery or technical assistance will be made in the form of goods--generally goods produced as a result of the industrial co-operation contract but in some cases, goods not directly related to the contract.
> . . . This form of payment in goods raises special financial problems.  In cases where the goods are not the same type as those comprised in the industrial co-operation contract itself, the party receiving them frequently finds it difficult to dispose of them and in some cases may even be obliged to use financial or trading intermediaries who may resell the goods or re-export them to buyers in other countries.  This practice frequently has adverse effects on existing exports of such goods and adds to the cost of the imports envisaged under the industrial co-operation contract.  But even in cases where the goods to be delivered are those produced as a result of the industrial co-operation contract, special financial problems also frequently exist because there is often a considerable time-gap between the deliveries on each side and because the sums involved are usually substantial.[32]

## MOST-FAVORED-NATION TREATMENT

The gradually emerging relationship between U.S.-based multinational corporations and the Eastern European socialist economies can also be impeded by domestic political developments in the United States.  More specifically, the 1974 domestic debates surrounding the extension of MFN treatment by the United States to the Soviet Union and socialist Eastern Europe, and the controversy surrounding the role of Eximbank created an atmosphere that, at least in the short run, is not conducive to the development of closer economic ties. The Control Data venture in Romania notwithstanding, most U.S.-based multinationals are, in some form, affected by these issues and, consequently, may display a more cautious attitude than they would if conditions were different. The controversy naturally also influences the attitudes of the Eastern European socialist governments. While they are anxious to obtain the advanced technology developed and controlled by U.S.-based multinational corporations, they consider U.S. government trade policies discriminatory and, consequently, formulate their own economic policies accordingly.

Because the problems are political in nature it is very difficult to predict what might happen in the future. World and U.S. domestic political conditions can easily change and, thus, rapidly create a more or less conducive atmosphere for the development of closer economic ties between U.S.-based multinationals and the Eastern European socialist economies. The current outlook seems favorable. In the spring of 1974, for example, several mixed U.S. trade missions of government officials and business executives visited Eastern Europe in general and Hungary in particular. Their purpose was to get acquainted with people and economic conditions and to seek out potential business opportunities. It is interesting to note that despite the controversies discussed before, multinationals were well represented in the group. Among others, Pfizer, Sperry Univac, ITT, Union Carbide, and Rockwell International Corporations sent top executives.[33]

SUMMARY

Increased East-West industrial cooperation in general, and closer economic ties between multinational corporations and the Eastern European socialist economies in particular, are impeded by a host of factors. In addition to the problems identified by the UN Economic Commission for Europe, such as lack of good information and financing, the several other problems identified can be classified in two major categories. The first category includes those problems, such as global political uncertainty and the absence of the MFN treatment by the United States, over which neither multinationals nor the socialist economies have control. Such problems are created and/or settled by the United

States and the Soviet Union, the two major representatives of the Western and socialist worlds. The second category includes those problems over which both multinational corporations and the socialist economies exert varying degrees of control. The inflexible socialist economic and administrative structures and rather rigid multinational ownership policies are good illustrations of this category. Problems in the second category can be handled by the Eastern European socialist economies and the multinational corporations in a reasonable and amicable way.[34] This proposition is, of course, predicated on the assumption that both the socialist economies and the multinationals are willing to reduce the currently existing mutual lack of trust to a more acceptable level. This is not to say that a completely trusting relationship can be developed-- such a relationship does not even exist between business firms within the Western world and between countries within the socialist camp. Multinational corporations are the most important business organizations in the capitalist world and the socialist economies represent an ideology that is alien to these organizations. Consequently, there are fundamental philosophical differences and, therefore, there are sound reasons for some mutual distrust. However, in view of the realities of economic life in both East and West, and in view of the substantial benefits that both multinationals and the socialist economies can obtain through closer ties, such mutual distrust should be and can be reduced to a level where it would interfere less with the gradually emerging relationships.

## NOTES

1. It is, of course, possible that in the future, Western Europe-based multinationals may also be under more stringent controls by the EEC. See Commission of the.European Communities, Multinational Undertakings and Community Regulations (Brussels, November 7, 1973).
2. Business International Eastern Europe Report, February 22, 1974, p. 53; and June 28, 1974, pp. 197-98.
3. The New York Times, March 10, 1974, p. E-6.
4. Business International Eastern Europe Report, September 21, 1974, p. 279.
5. Ibid., p. 280.
6. Ibid.
7. UN Economic Commission for Europe, Analytical Report on Industrial Cooperation Among ECE Countries (E/ECE/844), March 14, 1973, pp. 31-32.

8.  Ibid., p. 32.

9.  Ibid.

10. Die Zeit, March 22, 1974, p. 19.

11. Business International Eastern Europe Report, April 20, 1973, pp. 109-10.

12. UN Economic Commission for Europe, op. cit., p. 34.

13. As reported by Richard D. Robinson in International Business Management (New York: Holt, Rinehart and Winston, 1973), pp. 377.

14. Ibid.

15. See, for example, Nicolas Spulber, Socialist Management and Planning: Topics in Comparative Socialist Economies (Bloomington, Ind.: Indiana University Press, 1971).

16. Business Week, December 1, 1973, p. 44.

17. Business International Eastern Europe Report, September 21, 1973 and February 22, 1974, pp. 273-74 and 50-51, respectively.

18. Ibid., March 22, 1974, p. 90.

19. Robert S. Kretschmar, Jr. and Robin Foor, The Potential for Joint Ventures in Eastern Europe (New York: Praeger, 1972).

20. As described by Richard D. Robinson in International Business Management: A Guide to Decision-Making (New York: Holt, Rinehart and Winston, 1973), p. 327.

21. Ibid., pp. 327-28.

22. Ibid., p. 345.

23. Ibid., p. 343.

24. Ibid., p. 354-55.

25. United Nations, Secretariat and ST/ECA/190, Multinational Corporations in World Development (New York: United Nations, 1973), p. 41.

26. Business International Eastern Europe Report, March 22, 1974, p. 83.

27. From an interview given to Business Week, December 1, 1973, p. 44. See also John B. Holt, "New Roles for Western Multinationals in Eastern Europe," Columbia Journal of World Business, Fall 1973, pp. 131-39.

28. "U.S. Businessmen, Financiers Urged to Join Ventures," Commerce Today, October 28, 1974, p. 26.

29. Chase World Information Corporation, East-West Markets, March 25, 1974, p. 3.

30. Richard D. Robinson, op. cit., p. 354.

31. UN Economic Commission for Europe, op. cit., pp. 33-34.

32. Ibid., p. 33.

33. The Washington Post, April 11, 1974, p. C-14.

34. For a discussion of the gradually changing owner-ship strategies of multinational corporations, for example, see "New Era for Multinationals," Business Week, July 6, 1974, pp. 73-74.

# 5

## CONCLUSION

The development of close economic ties between multi-national corporations and the Eastern European socialist economies depends on the willingness and ability of multi-nationals to expand operations and on the general economic conditions in the socialist countries. As shown in the previous chapters, during the last 15-20 years, multina-tional corporations evolved as powerful business organiza-tions that are far more flexible than their predecessors were during the era of European imperialism. Moreover, during the same time the Eastern European socialist econ-omies have reached a stage of economic development and political flexibility where they are able to provide incen-tives, especially in the form of potential markets, that can motivate multinationals to develop closer ties through-out the region.

The rapid growth of multinational corporations during the late 1950s and during the decade of the 1960s came about under the leadership of American management that--detached from ownership--substituted sales maximization in conjunction with risk aversion for profit maximization as the single most important corporate objective. The rapid growth of multinationals was facilitated by the gradual lifting of trade barriers and by the increasing ability of international financial markets to accommodate large capital flows. As a result, by the early 1970s mul-tinational corporations emerged as the most powerful busi-ness organizations in the world economy. They are not bound, to any significant extent, by the economic or for-eign policy interests of nation states. At the same time, due to their advanced technology and control over world-wide marketing channels, multinational corporations have become the major vehicle for economic development.

Although the major political and economic features of the Eastern European socialist economies are similar, they no longer represent a monolithic political and economic block. The governments of Bulgaria, Czechoslovakia, the German Democratic Republic, Hungary, Poland, and Romania conduct a foreign policy that is in accord with that of the Soviet Union but still exhibits, to varying degrees, elements of independence (for example, Romania). The socialist countries also show disparities in the levels of economic development and income. From the largely agricultural-based economy of Bulgaria with a per capita income of $740 (1972), the level of development rises to that of the highly industrialized German Democratic Republic with a 1972 per capita income of $2,200. The degree of openness of the economies also varies; exports as a percentage of national income range from a low of 11 percent for Poland to a high of 43 percent for Bulgaria. Viewed as a group, these countries, as of 1972, represented an important market of approximately 104 million people with a median per capita income of $1,300 and accounted for $36 billion or 12 percent of world trade. However, 60 percent of this trade was within the framework of the Council of Mutual Economic Assistance so that the openness of the economies to the West has been limited.

To date, multinational corporations have not been very active in the Eastern European socialist economies. This is not the result of an accidental oversight on the part of either side, but the product of differing economic systems. Multinationals represent the most highly developed form of capitalist business organizations. The Eastern European socialist economies, on the other hand, are all centrally planned economies whose operating base is made up of state-owned industrial and commercial enterprises. Under such conditions, until recently, there was no ideologically justifiable and economically feasible role in socialist Eastern Europe for multinational corporations.

Three developments, however, have fundamentally changed the situation. First, the switch of the Eastern European socialist economies from extensive to intensive economic growth strategies. Second, the resulting economic reforms throughout the Eastern European region. Third, the recognition on the part of multinational corporations that through their own interaffiliate system of trade and payments they can subjugate national trade and payment barriers.

The current economic growth strategies of the Eastern European socialist economies are based on increased produc-

tivity rather than on new kinds of productive activity.
This is not simply a question of increasing labor productivity, although, given the relatively full utilization of
Eastern European labor forces and their anticipated slow
growth rate, this is a major consideration. More important,
the new strategies require the infusion of advanced technologies and the manufacture of quality products meeting
international standards. To help achieve these goals,
every Eastern European socialist government introduced economic reforms, some of them, such as the one in Hungary,
comprehensive, others, such as in Bulgaria and Czechoslovakia, more limited. The reforms have helped to promote
a more efficient allocation of resources. However, they
have not gone far enough to help close the competitive gap
with the highly industrialized Western economies, nor have
they given reasonable assurance that this gap can be closed
within the foreseeable future. Nevertheless, the degree
of change has generally been such that with certain guarantees, it is now conceivable that in selected sectors of
the socialist economies multinational corporations can suc-
cessfully carry on business operations. The extent of
their involvement, of course, depends on the Eastern European governments' perceived need for close economic ties
with such corporations.

In recent years, multinational corporations have become aware of their potential to transcend national trade
and exchange controls through their own worldwide interaffiliate trade and payment system. As the Eastern European
socialist economies are still largely insulated from international economic developments by production and price
controls as well as by an extensive system of exchange and
trade controls, multinational corporations are in a much
better position to develop closer ties with the socialist
economies than other types of Western business organizations. Generally, any trade and payment link between a
socialist country with extensive controls and a convertible currency area is sufficient to enable most multinational
corporations to engage in profitable operations. The most
useful link--from the viewpoint of both sides--is some form
of investment with an export component. In such cases,
most socialist countries, but especially Romania and Hungary, are very accommodating in that they guarantee that
approved profits, interests, and other convertible exchange
obligations are met promptly. Because of the inconverti-
bility of the Eastern European socialist currencies and
the extensive exchange controls in these countries, there
is no need for the socialist governments to worry about

the larger question of the role of multinational corporations in disequilibrating capital flows and in other developments associated with the reform of the international monetary systems.

Thus the potential for close economic ties between multinational corporations and the Eastern European socialist economies is substantial. The markets are there, skilled labor is available, and the economic environments, in most cases, are tolerable. Yet, the development of such ties is marked by slow progress. To some extent this is due--on the part of both sides--to the lack of knowledge on how to develop such ties and to the bureaucratic red tape involved in negotiations with the Eastern European countries. Over and above this, however, the Eastern European socialist economies in their project proposals to multinational corporations generally insist on the transfer of the most advanced technology and on the continuous updating of the same. Furthermore, most of the proposals call for the long-term involvement of multinational corporations. In line with their traditional ownership (that is, control) strategies most multinationals, however, are reluctant to take on long-term commitments involving the continuous transfer of advanced technology without a majority ownership position.

The policy of most multinational corporations to obtain close to 100 percent ownership in international ventures arises from the comparative advantage that such corporations have in management and/or proprietary technology that could be compromised if a minority ownership position were accepted. On the other hand, for political and ideological reasons most Eastern European socialist economies (the case of Romania and Hungary notwithstanding) have difficulties permitting even minority equity ownership by capitalist corporations. Thus, an apparent conflict is created.

Majority ownership and control, however, need not be synonymous, particularly in the Eastern European socialist economies. On the part of the Eastern European governments the benefits of majority ownership can be obtained through agreements enforced via regular and thorough monitoring of all activities of multinational corporations. On the other hand, multinational corporations can accept a minority ownership position even if they have comparative advantage in management and/or proprietary technology as long as the joint venture agreement provides for management control and for procedures that would secure control of proprietary technology. Consequently, if in principle an agreement can be reached, there is no reason why the Eastern European socialist economies and multinational corporations could not establish mutually beneficial long-range economic ties. The emergence of large-scale, long-term projects, such as the Control Data venture in Romania, lends support to the idea that this joint venture concept is gradually being adopted by both the socialist governments and multinational corporations.[1]

Another limiting factor is the conflicting nature of project objectives. In recent years multinational corporations have tried to extend their product life cycles through selling dated technology to developing countries. While some dated technology might be useful to the Eastern European socialist economies, most socialist governments want to acquire the most advanced technology together with a guarantee of the continuous updating of the same. Recently, multinational corporations have also tried to shift the production of labor intensive products to low labor-cost economies. While on the basis of the available (although limited) evidence it is reasonable to argue that labor costs in the Eastern European socialist economies are lower than in the highly industrialized economies of the West, large-scale labor intensive projects may no longer be entirely justified due to the increasingly tight socialist labor markets and the use of the "export wage" policies by some of the socialist governments. Based on this, it appears that in order to avoid conflicting objectives and the resulting problems, projects should involve the transfer of advanced technology that yields labor savings as well as products that can be competitive in both CMEA and world markets.

To date, only a limited number of such projects exist. Their future development rests on the ability of the Eastern European socialist economies to maintain high economic growth rates. For the decade of the 1970s the UN Economic Commission for Europe projected an average annual real growth rate of 5 percent for the region. It seems, in light of recent experience, that this estimate is unrealistically high. Nevertheless, in comparative terms the real growth rate of the Eastern European socialist economies can be expected to be somewhat higher than that of the highly industrialized Western economies. On the other hand, it appears that the insulation of the Eastern European socialist economies from international economic developments might also increase. According to the 1974-75 plans, inflation imported into socialist Eastern Europe from the West is going to be absorbed through subsidies, leaving domestic prices largely unchanged.[2]  To some extent, this is possible because a large part of energy and raw material imports come from the Soviet Union under long-term fixed price contracts valid until the end of 1975. In view of the continually increasing trade with the West, the Eastern European socialist governments, however, cannot continue to isolate their economies from long-term international economic developments.  Stopgap measures to keep price increases in the 2 to 5 percent range while world prices are increasing at the annual rate of 10 to 15 percent can only further distort basic economic relationships in the socialist countries.  Because of the very slow and uncertain process of international involvement by the Eastern European socialist economies it is likely that multinational corporations are going to continue to be wary of projects that do not involve the direct earning of convertible currencies.

In spite of the problems impeding the development of close ties, it can be expected that the increased interest evidenced by multinationals in the Eastern European region during the last two to three years is going to continue. The extent of their involvement, however, depends largely on the ability of the Eastern European socialist economies to provide and guarantee an economic environment in which the business activities of multinationals are not unduly hampered.

## NOTES

1.  J. Paul Lyet, chief executive officer of Sperry-Rand Corporation stated the concept very succinctly when he said that "thirty-five per cent of something is a lot better than 100% of nothing."  "New Era for Multinationals," Business Week, July 6, 1974, p. 74.

2.  Dusko Doder, "Eastern Europe's Inflation Stopgap," Herald Tribune International, July 15, 1974, p. 6.

DECREE OF THE MINISTER OF FINANCE [OF HUNGARY]
ON ECONOMIC ASSOCIATIONS
WITH FOREIGN PARTICIPATION

For implementing the  §31 of the Law-Decree No 19 of 1970
on economic associations /hereinafter:  Law-Decree/, I
decree, in agreement with the Minister of Foreign Trade,
the Minister of Labour and the President of the National
Bank of Hungary, as follows:

§1

Hungarian economic organisations, enumerated in §1 /1/ of
the Law-Decree any foreign enterprises or juridical persons may establish economic associations in Hungary, as
prescribed in  §2 of this Decree /hereinafter:  Association/
in the form of unlimited liability partnership, company
limited by shares, limited liability company and joint
enterprise.

§2

/1/ An Association may be established on basis of the
    parties' mutual interests for developing the level of
    technology and that of economy, for carrying on prof-
    itable trading and servicing activities.
/2/ The economic relations of the Association with Hungar-
    ian producing enterprises are governed by contracts,
    other than the memorandum of association.

§3

/1/ The memorandum of association, the articles of associa-
    tion, etc. /hereinafter:  memorandum of association/
    and any amendments thereof are effective with the ap-
    proval of the Minister of Finance.
/2/ The approval of the memorandum of association does not
    exempt from the obligation to acquire such licences
    of the authorities as are prescribed by statutory rules.

/3/ The application for approval should contain all the data, necessary for determining, whether the activities of the Association can be expected to realize the aims, laid down in  §2 above.

§4

The partners shall determine their contribution as prescribed by the statutory rules relating to the Association. In the total sum of the contributions /share capital, etc./, to be fixed in monetary terms, the participation of the foreign partner /s/ should generally not exceed 49 per cent.

§5

The Association is obliged to set aside a Risk Fund from its profits, as stipulated in the memorandum of association. The Risk Fund shall continuously be increased year by year until its sum will be equal to 10 per cent of the capital of the Association.

§6

/1/ The Association may set aside an Employees' Participation Fund to the debit of its annual profits, remaining after the sum of the Risk Fund has been deducted. The annual amount of the Employees' Participation Fund shall not exceed 15 per cent of the total wages, paid by the Association in that year.

/2/ The fixing of wages for the employees of the Association shall be governed by the memorandum of association and the contracts of employment, respectively, within the limits of the statutory rules and the approval, mentioned in §3.

§7

/1/ The Association is obliged to pay Profit Tax.

/2/ Profit Tax is to be reckoned on the basis of the annual profits of the Association, reduced by the sums to be set aside for the Risk Fund and the Employees' Participation Fund.

/3/ The rate of the Profit Tax is 40 per cent on profits, not exceeding 20 percent of the capital of the Association and 60 per cent, exceeding these profits.

/4/ In case the Association utilises its taxes profits for increasing its assets, a part of the Profit Taxes,

126

paid on such profits, may be refunded upon special application, submitted to the Ministry of Finance.

§8

Employees of foreign nationality of the Association may transfer abroad 50 per cent of any kind of their incomes, paid by the Association, in a currency, stipulated in the memorandum of association.

§9

/1/ The Association is exempt from levies on its tied-up assets, from paying up the centralized portion of the depreciation allowance and from the wage-development levies.

/2/ In respect of other taxes and obligations of tax nature of the Association, including the social security and pension contributions, the provisions of the Hungarian statutory rules are to be applied.

§10

/1/ The operations of the Association, connected with foreign currencies and exchanges shall be reckoned in accordance with regulations, applicable to the Hungarian economic organisations.

/2/ The Association may raise credits in accordance with regulations, applicable to the Hungarian economic organisations.

§11

/1/ The National Bank of Hungary /hereinafter: the Bank/ will transfer abroad, to the extent of the sum paid up to the Bank, in favour of the foreign partner the profits and any sums due to the foreign partner in a currency, stipulated in the memorandum of association.

/2/ The Bank, on application of the foreign partner, submitted simultaneously with the approval of the memorandum of association, /in accordance with the document of approval / §3// may guarantee a compensation for damages, resulting from acts of the State, if any, relating to the foreign partner's contribution, effected up to the amount of that contribution.

/3/ For the obligations of the Association, resulting from the partnership, the Bank or the Hungarian Foreign

Trade Bank Ltd. may undertake guarantee towards the
foreign partner, according to the usual terms of banking practice.

/4/ In case of the withdrawal of the foreign partner, the
Bank transfers abroad the foreign partner's share, due
in proportion to its contribution, to the extent of
the sum paid up to the Bank in a currency, stipulated
in the memorandum of association.

/5/ While implementing international agreements on double
taxation, the standpoint of the Minister of Finance
is decisive in the question of reciprocity.

## §12

/1/ The annual losses of the Association are to be charged
against the Risk Fund.

/2/ Should the Risk Fund not cover the losses and the partners do not settle the losses otherwise, the Minister
of Finance decides as to the further activity or winding up of the Association.

/3/ Should the Association become insolvent and its liabilities exceed its assets, the Minister of Finance or-
ders the winding up of the Association.

/4/ In the cases referred to under a line as /2/ and /3/,
the receiver will be appointed by the Minister of Finance.

/5/ Should the Association be wound up for reasons, stipulated in the memorandum of association, or else upon
the partners' decision, the winding up is to be carried
out in accordance with the statutory rules, applying
to the associations.

## §13

In case of winding up of the Association the foreign share,
remaining after the liabilities of the Association having
been settled, may be transferred abroad tax-free, in a
currency stipulated in the memorandum of association.

## §14

/1/ This Decree comes into force on the day of its promul-
gation; its rules are to be applied to Associations,
established subsequent to coming into force of this
Decree.

/2/ The Association may carry on its activities on the basis of the rules of the Laws No's XXXVII of 1875 and V

of 1930 relating to unlimited liability partnership, company limited by shares and limited liability company, respectively, as are kept in force by the Annex of the Law-Decree No 11 of 1960 and on the basis of the Law-Decree No 19 of 1970 as well as according to rules of the present Decree.

/3/ Associations under this Decree are exempted from the Decree of the Minister of Finance No 21 of 1961 /XI.30./ PM.

/4/ This Decree does not apply to matters, settled by international agreements.

Lajos Faluvegi m.p.<br>
Minister of Finance

# BIBLIOGRAPHY

## BOOKS

Adam, Gyorgy. <u>Amerika Europaban: Vallalatbirodalmak a Vilaggazdasagban</u> (<u>America in Europe: Corporate Empires in the World Economy</u>). Budapest: Akademiai Konyvkiado, 1970.

_____. <u>The World Corporation Problematics: Apologetics and Critique</u>. Budapest: Hungarian Scientific Council for World Economy, 1971.

_____. <u>Vilagkonszernek: Valogatas</u> (<u>World Corporations: A Book of Readings</u>). Budapest: Kozgazdasagi es Jogi Konyvkiado, 1974.

Ausch, Sandor. <u>Theory and Practice of CMEA Cooperation</u>. Budapest: Academic Publishing House, 1972.

Beard, Miriam. <u>A History of Business</u>. Ann Arbor, Mich.: Ann Arbor Paperback, 1962 (reprint).

Brabant, van Jozef M. P. <u>Bilateralism and Structural Bilateralism in Intra-CMEA Trade</u>. Rotterdam: University Press, 1973.

Dunning, J. H. <u>The Multinational Enterprise</u>. London: Allen and Unwin, 1971.

Gott, Sidney. <u>The GATT Negotiations, 1973-75: A Guide to the Issues</u>. Montreal: British North American Committee, April 1974.

Hymer, Stephen. <u>The International Operations of National Firms, A Study of Direct Investment</u>. Unpublished Ph.D. dissertation, Massachusetts Institute of Technology, 1960.

Kretschmar, Robert S., Jr., and Robin Foor. <u>The Potential for Joint Ventures in Eastern Europe</u>. New York: Praeger, 1972.

Lauter, Geza Peter.  The Manager and Economic Reform in
    Hungary.  New York:  Praeger, 1972.

Mastrapasqua, Frank.  U.S. Expansion via Foreign Branching:
    Monetary Policy Implications.  New York:  New York Uni-
    versity Press, 1973.

McMillan, C. H., and D. P. St. Charles.  Joint Ventures in
    Eastern Europe:  A Three-Country Comparison.  Montreal:
    C. D. Howe Research Institute, 1973.

Rich, E. F.  Hudson's Bay Company 1670-1870.  Toronto:
    McClelland and Stewart, 1960.

Robinson, Richard D.  International Business Management.
    New York:  Holt, Rinehart and Winston, 1973.

Sampson, Anthony.  The Sovereign State of ITT.  New York:
    Stein and Day, 1973.

Selucky, Radoslav.  Economic Reforms in Eastern Europe:
    Political Background and Economic Significance.  New
    York:  Praeger, 1972.

Sinanian, Sylvia, Istvan Deak, and Peter C. Ludz, eds.
    Eastern Europe in the 1970's.  New York:  Praeger, 1972.

Spulber, Nicolas.  Socialist Management and Planning:
    Topics in Comparative Socialist Economies.  Blooming-
    ton, Ind.:  Indiana University Press, 1971.

Turner, Louis.  Multinational Corporations and the Third
    World.  New York:  Hill and Wang, 1973.

Wells, H. G.  The Outline of History.  New York:  Garden
    City Books, 1961.

Wolf, Thomas A.  East-West Economic Relations and the Mul-
    tinational Corporation, Occasional Paper No. 5.  Wash-
    ington, D.C.:  Center for Multinational Studies, July
    1973.


                        ARTICLES

Adam, Gyorgy.  "A nemzetkozi vallalatbirodalmak globalis
    optimilizalasanak ujabb fe jlemenyei" ("New Develop-

                          131

ments in the Global Optimization of the International Corporate Empires"). Kozgazdasagi Szemle (Economic Review), July-August 1972, pp. 944-58.

_____. "Problems of Inter-Firm Cooperation Between East and West," unpublished paper presented to the Third International Conference on Corporate Planning in Brussels, Belgium, September 17-19, 1973.

_____. "Szokeveny iparagak es elvandorlo vallalatok a tokes vilaggazdasagban" ("Runaway Industries and Relocating Corporations in the Capitalistic World-Economy"). Kozgazdasagi Szemle (Economic Review), September-October 1971, pp. 1066-81, 1185-1203.

Baranson, Jack. "Technology Transfer Through the International Firm." American Economic Review, May 1970, p. 438.

Business International Eastern Europe Report, November 17, 1972; December 1, 1972; December 15, 1972; February 23, 1973; March 9, 1973; March 23, 1973; April 6, 1973; April 20, 1973; May 18, 1973; June 15, 1973; August 10, 1973; September 27, 1973; November 2, 1973; December 7, 1973; January 11, 1974; January 25, 1974; February 8, 1974; February 22, 1974; March 22, 1974; June 28, 1974.

Business Week, December 1, 1973; March 9, 1974; July 6, 1974.

Der Spiegel, February 11, 1974.

Die Zeit, March 8, 1974; March 22, 1974.

Donaghue, Hugh P. "Control Data's Joint Venture in Romania." Columbia Journal of World Business, December 1973, pp. 83-89.

East-West Markets (publication of Chase World Information Corporation), March 25, 1974; July 29, 1974.

Electronics Weekly, June 13, 1973, p. 17.

Figyelo, February 21, 1973; August 1, 1973; September 12, 1973; October 3, 1973; October 10, 1973; October 24, 1973; February 6, 1974; April 17, 1974.

Fortune, no. 3 (September 1973), p. 164.

Gaedeke, Ralph M. "Selected U.S. Multinational Service Firms in Perspective." Journal of International Business Studies, Spring 1973.

Gazdasagi Kutato Intezet (Economic Research Institute). "A nagy ipari vallalatokrol" ("About Large Industrial Enterprises"). Gazdasag (Economics), December 1973, pp. 76-92.

Heininger, Horst. "The Impact of Multinational Corporations on International Economic and Political Relations," unpublished paper. Berlin, GDR: Institute for International Politics and Economics, 1973.

Herald Tribune International, July 15, 1974.

Holt, John B. "New Roles for Western Multinationals in Eastern Europe." Columbia Journal of World Business, Fall 1973, pp. 131-39.

Kudlinski, Romuald. "Some Problems of the Multinational Corporations: A Few Sidenotes on the Report Issued by the U.N. Department of Economic and Social Affairs," unpublished paper. Warsaw, Poland: Institute for Economic Sciences, University of Warsaw, 1973.

Mason, Hal R. "The Multinational Firm and the Cost of Technology to Developing Countries." California Management Review, Summer 1973, p. 13.

Nehls, Dr. habil. Katja. "Internationale Konzerne--Monopolmacht, Klassenkampf." IPW-Forschungshefte, Institut fur Internationale Politik und Wirtschaft, GDR, 8. Jahrgang, Heft 1/1973.

Nepszabadsag (People's Freedom), September 22, 1968.

New York Times, September 22, 1973; March 10, 1974.

Quinn, James Brian. "Technology Transfer by Multinational Companies." Harvard Business Review, November-December 1969, p. 150.

Robuck, Stefan H., and Kenneth Simonds. "International Business: How Big Is It? The Missing Measurements."

*Columbia Journal of World Business*, May-June 1970, pp. 6-19.

Washington *Post*, November 11, 1973; April 11, 1974.


PUBLIC DOCUMENTS

Commission of the European Communities. *Multinational Undertakings and Community Regulations*. Brussels, November 7, 1973.

General Agreement on Tariffs and Trade. *GATT Activities in 1972*. Geneva, 1973.

_____. *GATT Information*, GATT/1133. Geneva, September 1973.

United Nations. *Multinational Corporations in World Development* (ST/ECA/190). New York, 1973.

_____, Economic and Social Council. *The Impact of Multinational Corporations on the Development Process and on International Relations* (E/5500), June 12, 1974.

_____, Economic Commission for Europe. *Analytical Report on Industrial Co-operation Among ECE Countries* (E/ECE/844), May 4, 1973.

United States, Senate Committee on Finance. *The Multinational Corporations and the World Economy* (Washington, D.C.: U.S. Government Printing Office, 1973).

_____, Department of Commerce, Bureau of East-West Trade. *Selected U.S.S.R. and Eastern European Economic Data*, June 1973.

international organization;
  International Monetary
  Fund, 14, 38; General
  Agreement on Tariffs and
  Trade, 12-14, 37-38; United
  Nations, 16; UN "Group of
  Eminent Persons," 16
international saving, 76-77
investment environment; administrative inflexibility,
  103-05; labor, stability
  and quality, 61-64; market
  indicators, 66, 67; politi-
  cal-economic conditions,
  60-61; production costs,
  64-65; technology, 68-73

joint ventures, 104, 106,
  111; contractual, 56; equity, 36, 58, 59, 77, 89-90,
  105, 108-16

labor, 1-2, 9, 18, 61-64;
  East European labor unions,
  63; internationalization of
  unions, 62-63
licensing agreements, 56

market potential, 66
marketing, 1, 82-86, 87
multinational corporations;
  access to markets, 82-86;
  benefits for Eastern Europe, 73-87; capital, 15,
  80-81; definition, viii;
  East European views concerning, 39-50; expansion
  pattern, 8-10; government
  relations, 4, 6; growth, 6;
  history, 2-4; host country
  relationship, 16-17, 18;
  Hudson's Bay Company, 3-4;

multinational corporations
  (cont'd)
  multinational sourcing, 76-
  77; imperialism, 2, 3-4;
  objectives, incompatibility
  with Eastern Europe, 109-
  16; ownership strategies,
  105-09; size, 6-8, 74; sovereign base, 6; technology,
  73, 78-80; theory of, 10-
  12; trade, 8; transfer
  pricing, 17; views of East
  Europeans, 39-50, 73

ownership strategies, 105-09

political climate, 60-61,
  94-97
product life-cycle, 11, 111
production costs, 64-65

remittances, dividend, and
  profits, 17
reserves, foreign exchange,
  15
risk, 10-12

service industries, 10
Special Drawing Rights, 14
subcontracting agreements, 56

tariffs, most-favored-nations
  clause, 13, 95, 114
technology, 68-73; multinational, 78-80; transfer
  method, 10
trade; bilateralism, 32, 35,
  37, 66-68, 88, 111; trade
  investment of Eastern Europe, 22, 24-25; intra-CMEA,
  32-35; nontariff barriers,
  13, 113; theory, 1-2
transfer pricing, 17

GEZA P. LAUTER is on the faculty of the School of Government and Business Administration of the George Washington University in Washington, D.C. He studied and worked in Hungary for many years and lived also in England, Canada, and Turkey, where he spent three years with Cornell University under a Cornell-Agency for International Development contract.

Dr. Lauter received a B.A. in languages in Budapest, Hungary, in 1954. His further studies include a B.A. in economics and an MBA and Ph.D. in Management from the University of California at Los Angeles in 1964 and 1968, respectively. He is the author, among others, of The Manager and Economic Reform in Hungary (Praeger, 1972).

PAUL M. DICKIE is a senior economist with the International Monetary Fund in Washington, D.C., and teaches part-time at George Washington University in the area of multinational business policy. A Canadian national, he received his B.A.Sc. in Chemical Engineering from the University of British Columbia in 1961. Postgraduate studies include an MBA and DBA in International Business and Finance from the University of Southern California in 1964 and 1968, respectively.

Dr. Dickie has held positions in private business, academeia and prior to his most recent position at the IMF, he was the Director of the Economics Branch, National Energy Board, Ottawa. His publications are mainly in the field of international finance and multinational business.

$770433258

**RELATED TITLES**

Published by

Praeger Special Studies

THE IMPACT OF U.S. INVESTMENT IN EUROPE:  A Case Study of
the Automotive and Computer Industries
>> Y. S. Hu; foreword by Christopher
>> Layton

TRADE RELATIONS OF THE EEC:  An Empirical Investigation of
the Enlarged European Community
>> Mordechai E. Kreinin

MANAGING FOREIGN INVESTMENT IN SOUTHERN ITALY:  U.S. Business in Developing Areas of the EEC
>> Douglas F. Lamont; with the special
>> assistance of Robert Purtshert; fore-
>> word by Eric N. Baklanoff

EAST-WEST BUSINESS TRANSACTIONS
>> Robert Starr

INDUSTRIAL MANAGEMENT:  EAST AND WEST
>> Edited by Aubrey Silberston and
>> Francis Seton

INTERNATIONAL CONTROL OF INVESTMENT:  The Dusseldorf Conference on Multinational Corporations
>> Edited by Don Wallace, Jr.; assisted
>> by Helga Ruof-Koch

MANAGING MULTINATIONAL CORPORATIONS
>> Arvind V. Phatak